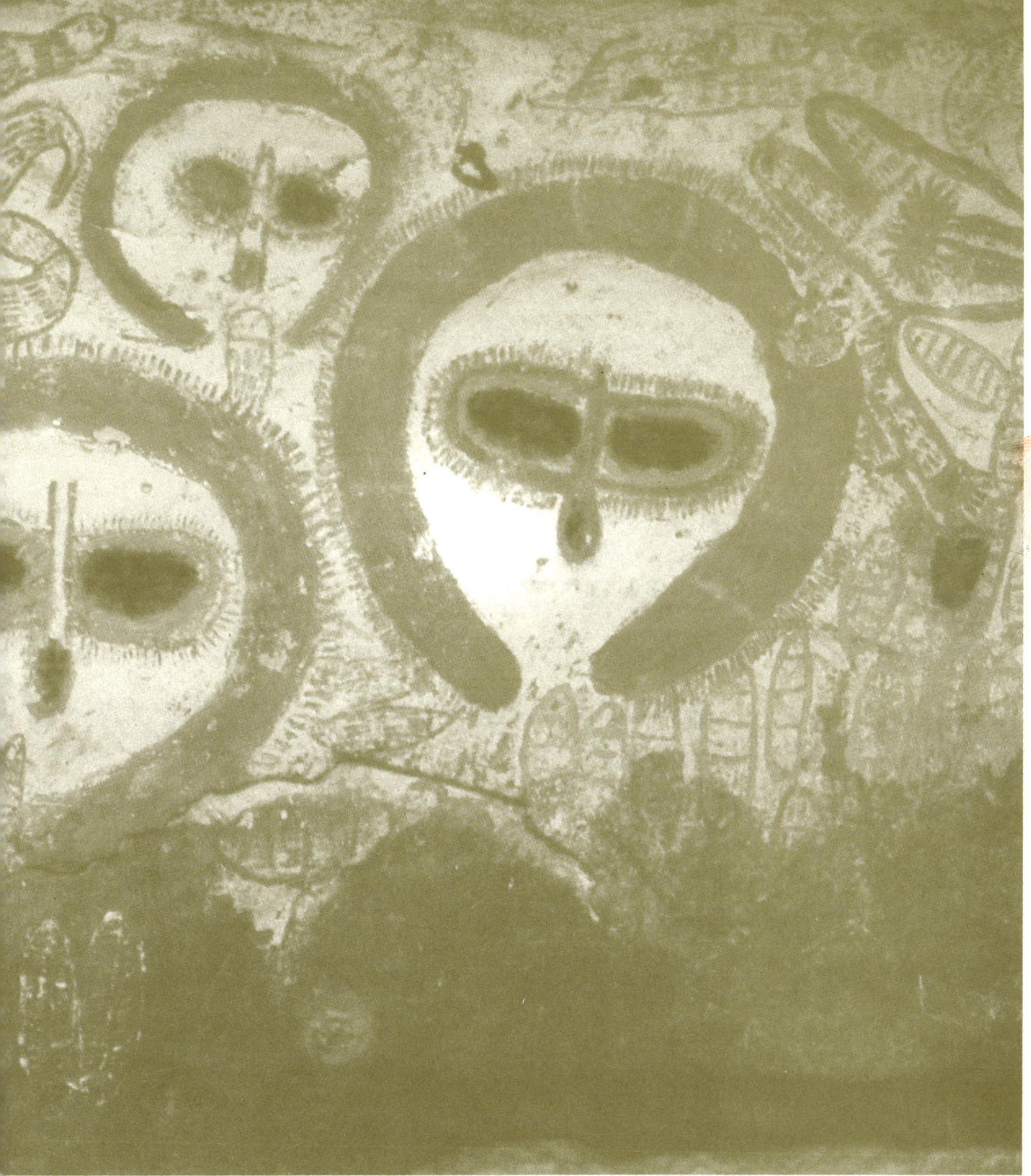

# ROCK PAINTINGS
## OF ABORIGINAL AUSTRALIA

# ROCK PAINTINGS

## OF ABORIGINAL AUSTRALIA

*Elaine Godden*
*Photography by Jutta Malnic*

REED

REED BOOKS PTY LTD
2 Aquatic Drive Frenchs Forest NSW 2086

*First published 1982*
*This edition published 1988*

National Library of Australia
Cataloguing-in-Publication Data:
Godden, Elaine
   Rock paintings of Aboriginal Australia.
   Bibliography.
   Includes index.
   ISBN 0 7301 0206 8

   1. Rock paintings — Australia. 2. Aborigines,
   Australia — Art. I. Malnic, Jutta. II. Title.
709'.01'130994

*Set by Pavilion Press Set, Sydney*
*printed and bound in Singapore*
*for Imago Production (FE) Pte Ltd*

# ACKNOWLEDGEMENTS

We are grateful for many peoples' help, given in a host of different ways. Most especially, and first, we thank Mowaljarlai, Jagamurro, Mirritji, Ngaleywan, Billy Munro, Jacob Burcu, Daisy Utemorrah, Rita and Bluey Howie and their families, especially Umbagun, Deluk, Jilgi and Scotty at Wah, Gibb River, Mowanjum, Meda and Napier Downs communities in Western Australia. Also Clifford and Desmond Coulthard of the Adnjamathana community, South Australia. If this book carried a dedication it would be to these people, particularly Mowaljarlai and Jagamurro who truly represent the seriousness and unbounded generosity of their people. In Cape York we were glad of the help of Stephen Trezise and Janelle, Percy Trezise and other people of the little community at Laura. Amanda Jones saved us from many things, including ourselves, in Cape York and the Centre: we could not do justice here to the worth of her company and help. In Alice Springs George Page-Sharp of the Northern Territory Conservation Commission gave us guidance, as did Ian Kaywood and Ian Marshall (in a very practical way) at Uluru. We thank Hilary and Derrick French for putting-us-up-with. In South Australia we also had valuable assistance from Rosemary Buchan, Lynton McGirr, Garry Simmons, David Simmons and K. P. Peterson. Victorians Betty and Rex Foster (Grampians) and Evelyn and Eric Barber (Glenisla) were of great help. As well as the Kimberley people mentioned first, we are grateful for the help of the other Western Australians: Lesley Corbett of Kimberley Land Council, Pat and Peter Lacey of Mt Elizabeth, Bishop Jobst of Broome and Stephen Hegerty and Barbara Thorn of Kunanurra. We thank Bob Moffatt of the National Parks and Wildlife Service in Cobar, Allen Fox of the National Parks and Wildlife Service in Canberra and Sharon Sullivan in Sydney. We are also grateful to Irml Mensdorff-Pouilly, Perpetua Hobcroft, John McLeod and Peter Burmeister. Wild-Leitz lent some special camera equipment which was of great help. Pamela Lofts was a pleasure to work and walk with in Kimberley; her support was of the most generous personal kind.

I would also like to gratefully acknowledge Alan Rumsey's valuable assistance with the Ngarinyin orthography.

The text of the book naturally draws on the published work of a number of academics and storytellers. This work is listed in the book's bibliography although it was not always possible to acknowledge it at precise points in the text. We are greatly and willingly in debt to John Clegg and Tia Negeravich who read the first draft of the manuscript. The value of the things they said was seen to be inestimable once initial shock had been dealt with. Lastly but most particularly we thank Don Godden, Sergei Malnic and Cass Godden for their support and patience.

# PREFACE

Colin Johnson has told me that the chief value of the words in this book, from his point of view, is that so many of them were spoken by Aboriginals. More exactly, he says that apart from examining the artistic tradition of the Aboriginal people from the European view, I have listened to the people whose heritage it is and who still produce artists in the tradition. I have done a lot of listening, never enough. Colin Johnson is a novelist, poet, historian; an Aboriginal whose art is in a different tradition from that talked about in this book because his recent Bibulman ancestors were forced from the places which generated and nurtured the older artistic ways. These and all the other aspects of Aboriginal culture are still his heritage, as they are the heritage of Aboriginal people all over Australia from the cities to the ragged fringes of country towns, from mission-founded settlements and vast graziers' properties to outstations where family groups hunt, paint and follow the old ceremonial and secular ways.

The words of just two people from very different lives preface this book and give an idea, at least, of what their heritage means to them. Larry Jakamarra Nelson speaks as a teacher of old traditions. His mother-tongue is Warlpiri: he spoke these words in English for the book and I wrote them down as he went. Some important words came in Warlpiri.

When I look at my *tjukurpa* [dreaming] paintings it makes me feel good — happy in *kuturu* [heart], spirit. Everything is there: all there in the caves, not lost. This is my secret side.

This is my home: inside me — *ngogunba* [mind] and *kuturu* — for *tjukurpa*. If I go away for a while I am unhappy — or if somebody dies. When I go back I am happy again.

Our dreaming; secret side: we must hold on to this, like our fathers, looking after it — all things, looking after them. We give to our sons when we die. The sons keep this from their fathers, grandfathers. The sons will remember, they can carry on, not be lost. And it is still there: fathers' country with rockhole, painted cave. We make outstations where the painted caves are. The people keep their ceremony things and pictures: they make them new. They bring young boys for learning to the caves: telling the stories, giving the laws from grandfathers' fathers, learning to do the paintings — *tjukurpa* way.

We can tell the European many things, looking after our secret side — not taking picture. *Mala* [hare-wallaby], *yalla* [yam], *ngalkari* [witchetty grub] — all made there. Nobody goes except after asking the owner: Jakamarra, Jungarai, Jampijinpa — they must be asked.

LARRY JAKAMARRA NELSON
Warlpiri people
Yuendumu,
Northern Territory

Long ago my skin itched as men entered my pores
And ran their fingers lightly along my walls,
Or scratched faintly diagrammatic lines.
From then on men and others touched me in other ways
The Wandjina ate themselves through my skin to become my very bones.
White, yellow-haloed figures with gapped eyes
Waited for the tribal dead and touching fingers of the living
Marking out the living.
In other places my skin was dotted and tapped and corroded by shapes;
Even the wraith-like Mimi emerged from between my cells
To mark a rock with stick-like figures of grace
Which men might copy or trace with wondering nails.
The dancing Quinkan quivered across my skin;
A hand was stencilled and a thylacine traced.
My flesh shivered with thousands of tracks and figures and signs —
To be followed by strange horrific shapes
And stranger men with stranger weapons,
To be etched and kept for all to see
That life was ever-changing across my skin.

COLIN JOHNSON
Bibulman people
Swan River, Western Australia
(Melbourne, Victoria)

# CONTENTS

# INTRODUCTION

This book illustrates and tells a little about some of the rock paintings and drawings in Australia. The pictures and places shown and discussed are a small part of a large subject, rock painting, which is part of a bigger subject, rock art. Rock art is in turn a small part of the whole of Aboriginal art. And artistic expression, although it encompasses so many of the things that people think and do, is still one of the many kinds of behaviour which form a society. Some of the things that are known about Australian Aboriginal societies, past and present, are set down here, especially if they relate to pictures on rock.

Pictures, like all other things, have no meaning outside people: those who make them and those who see them. The pictures in this book were made to be seen in the light of a set of consciously understood values by the people of the makers' societies. Now people from outside those societies are seeing them and making judgements about them. These judgements reflect different values and attitudes from those which produced the pictures and, since people believe that their own society's way of thinking and behaving is the right way, different ways must be wrong. The wrongness, in these terms, of Australian Aboriginal ways of making pictures was expressed for a time by outsiders as a refusal to accept the pictures as art at all and then by their designation as primitive art to distinguish them from proper art.

Early outside judgements on Aboriginal art were made by European specialists whose job it was to judge the art of their own societies. These people were part of an elite which dominated cultural and political institutions in their own societies and at whose instigation and on whose behalf modern colonialism had developed. They were arbiters of good taste in all the arts; they decided on behalf of their societies what was 'good' and 'bad', 'civilised' and 'primitive'. Other members of their societies had no need to consider what words such as *civilisation* or *art* meant or to realise that 'uncivilised' and 'primitive' people were a new version of the barbarians who had been set outside ancient Greek society because their languages, customs and beliefs were different from those of the Greeks. Neither need they know that the noun *art* had so recently been coined in order that the subject could be discussed according to a set of values which had grown up quickly in western society around the importance of *things*. Modern colonialism had brought Aboriginal art, among many other things from other places, to the attention of western art critics and historians; it and its makers were judged according to the values which had inspired their acquisition.

In the western world values were based on spiritual and religious considerations until the Renaissance. From the fifteenth century, more values began to be attached to material things. Trade expanded; money was needed to express the value of merchandise and new technology was needed to explore possible sources of more and different kinds of goods. In the sixteenth and seventeenth centuries great voyages of exploration were made but it was not until the following two centuries that technological innovations made possible the voyages of more and safer ships and the acquisition of commercial quantities of goods and of more territories on behalf of the rulers of European countries. The peoples of the claimed lands were part of the western colonial acquisition and so were their cultures and their products, including paintings and carvings.

It was advancing technology in the service of material gain which had brought the western peoples into real contact with other peoples and it was in terms of the values attaching to the acquisition of things that the other people were judged. They were found to be 'other': they did not place the same value on technology as western peoples did. Their values were different. They must also be wrong because, if they were not, then the rightness of western values might be challenged. The wrongness of the others' values — ways of life — was expressed in degrees of civilisation which were defined in terms of levels of technology. The western way stood alone as 'advanced civilisation' and others' ways were described as more or less civilised according to the amount of technology used in them. Societies valuing technology and material goods very little were considered uncivilised — even primitive. The Australians fell into this category and it was important to their conquerors that their material poverty be emphasised lest the real richness of their lives, expressed in complex religious beliefs, languages, ceremonies and structures of society and law, called into question the value of material gain as a social end.

But if the societies described as less civilised and primitive were of no value themselves to the western world, their products and their possessions, including their land, their labour and some of their manufactures, were most useful. Western artists were not long in using the fresh ideas of form shown in the art objects brought to their attention by the acquisition of foreign cultures. Western art was a commodity. It had begun changing its social role with the Renaissance and, by the eighteenth century, was no longer charged with expressing its societies' single religious idea. This no longer existed. There was scope for expressing any number of ideas and the manner in which they were expressed changed from time to time according to what was judged to be good, and therefore valuable, art. As fashions in good art changed so did the way in which subjects were expressed — the style. By the late nineteenth century the

European market for art objects was still expanding and many style changes had occurred. Artists were always alert for new forms of expression.

When new kinds of cultural property started flowing into Europe from its colonies, the items were at first treated as curios, proof of adventures in strange lands and the embodiment of titillating rumours of outrageous social behaviour. But European artists quickly realised that the art objects of other cultures represented a great reservoir of new forms, some of which they could, and did, adopt and adapt for their own use.

In Australia, the country had been claimed in the late eighteenth century on behalf of Britain's rulers and the owners of it had been found to place so little value on material possessions that their extreme 'otherness' had had them labelled 'primitive'. In time, some of the newcomers began to find positive use for Aboriginal ways. Ethnographers recorded information about how societies worked: they visited the people, asked them questions about their beliefs, their relationships, their diets and their rules and collected their utensils, weapons, ornaments and art objects. Artists among the newcomers made their art according to the European tradition, and the ethnographers' photographs, drawings and collections of Aboriginal art objects presented them with a rich array of new forms and ideas. Margaret Preston, Sidney Nolan and Clifton Pugh tapped this source quite early in Australia.

Margaret Preston admired Aboriginal art. From 1925 she began to point out that western artists had a great deal to learn from its linear style and the spareness of its techniques. She set herself the task of reducing her materials to match the range used by Aboriginal artists and of evolving a new Australian art from their techniques. At that time, she did not concern herself with the meanings of the forms she admired. Later she spoke of the 'inherent vision' of Aboriginal art and urged fellow artists to understand the subject. She was not referring to specific meanings of particular forms but simply acknowledging the world view expressed in all art and implying that Aboriginal art was as important as any other in this respect.

Those two new Australian specialist groups, artists and ethnographers (or anthropologists), differed in their appreciation of Aboriginal art. Artists valued its visual forms and did not concern themselves with their particular meanings. They were free to adapt its forms without espousing values which were unacceptable in their own society. The new specialist artists formed a small circle in Australian society and their activities concerned relatively few others. Anthropologists formed another small specialised group. They saw Aboriginal art in terms of its meaning, as part of the whole expression of its societies, and did not recognise for a long time that artists of their own society had attached positive value to its visual forms. Anthropologists continued until after the 1940s to defend what they understood to be the deficiencies of Aboriginal art — its differences from European art — as they defended whole Aboriginal value systems against what they increasingly came to see as unfair judgements of them according to European technological and material values.

Pictures are about people, and most books about Aboriginal art have been written from this anthropological viewpoint. Art can be analysed in terms of style — the material expression of the ideas it contains — just as social structure can be classified and analysed according to rules of kinship. But classifications are only ever set up to find out about other related things. Almost all Australian rock pictures were made by artists who are now dead, most of them long dead, and classifications of rock paintings and drawings have been set up to help us understand the past. Sequences of styles through time can suggest questions about change and migration, peoples' use of space can be investigated and these sorts of ideas can be related to other things that the archaeological record suggests were then happening in societies. This is a recent, outsider's, way of catching meaning. But many paintings express present peoples' ideas and values and form a link, tenuous as yet, with the older expressions as well as with other present expressions of the societies which produced them.

If we look at other peoples' pictures — or any of their things or actions — without trying to understand as well as we can the values which inspired them, we limit our knowledge and our appreciation of them. We not only trap ourselves in a limited view of the world which ill serves our present needs but, more importantly, we also trap others in the consequences of our ignorance.

# 1
# LISTENING
# TO THE PAST:
# PREHISTORY

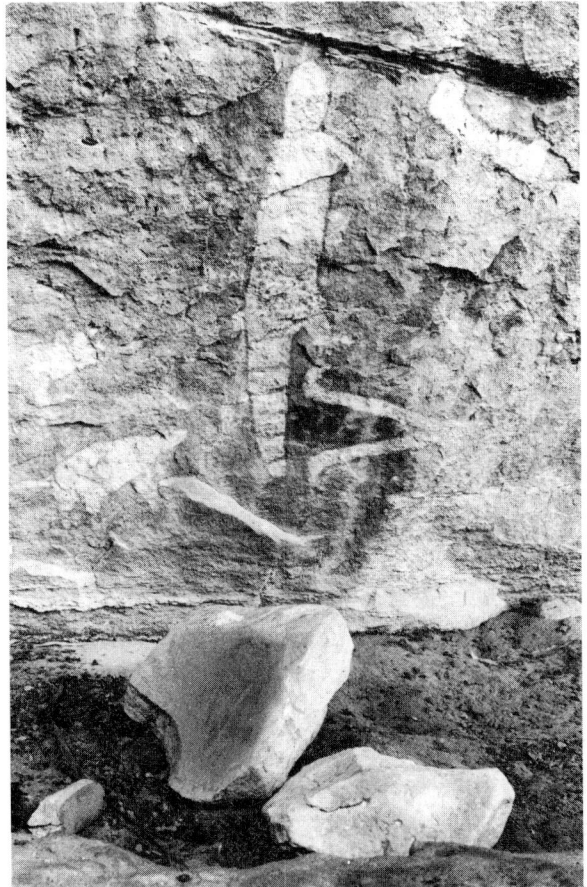

A painted shelter in Cape York with grindstones used for ochre on the floor.

Art speaks with two voices. One makes a simple statement of its existence in the world over tens of thousands of years of human history. The other, the voice of particular beliefs and values, fades to a whisper almost as soon as we begin to listen down the years. The noise of our own ignorance stops our ears to some of what we might otherwise hear, and simple imagination has often filled the silent spaces in our understanding. But people are freeing themselves from their own conventional attitudes, listening and looking harder and finding new ways to catch meaning from the past.

The voice we hear in reply to questions asked of people exists in the present although it draws on past events for the ideas and beliefs it expresses. Societies inherit and evolve useful meaning from different kinds of events without needing to separate them in terms of reality. Were the events of the Peloponnesian War more real than those leading to the banishment of Adam and Eve from the Garden of Eden? Could the reasons for the mighty battle between the Ngarinyin and Worora peoples be believed in more than those for which Memej brought the giant whirlwind to wrest the power of the *mayangarri* law stone from the Wongai women? It is not important as long as the meanings have some use to societies.

Ideas relate to events in at least two ways: the way in which the makers of the event understand they are related, and the way in which patterns contained in an event, or formed by numbers of events, suggest they are related. A person building a house will explain why it is that size and shape, facing in that direction and standing on that spot, but what the house explains about its builder's society's use of space can be seen by its place in a pattern formed by all the houses built around that time and in that neighbourhood. The pattern may be seen long after the house builder's death and even after the death of his society provided the houses or evidence of their position and form remains.

Archaeologists deal with the physical remains of people and their activities and hardly ever with the actual people who left them, although they may talk to the descendants of those people. But societies change: from time to time their members start doing things in new ways for new reasons. And the reasons the people themselves could give are only a conscious part of the meaning of what they do. In letting go of immediate, conscious meanings of actions and objects we can look at the patterns they form within and across space and time and get hold of different and broader kinds of meaning. These kinds of meaning are not more or less real than the other, often more conscious, kinds but they are the only kinds left when people who could explain their actions and manufactures are dead. But when is an idea dead? Perhaps only when all possible inheritors are dead. Otherwise, we can only guess at the relationship between present peoples' ideas about things and the ideas attached by their ancestors to things which seem, to us, very similar.

Although most of Australia's rock art is prehistoric, which only means that there is no record of its conscious meaning available, there are some pictures on rock which can still be explained by the descendants of their artists. Some of these people are charged with caring for and remaking pictures, a few have made pictures on rock in living memory, and many continue to make similar pictures with other materials such as bark. For many people in the north and centre of Australia rock art is part of their expression of life's meaning and can be explained in terms of what life presently means. Since we have no way of knowing how, or even whether, ideas about a picture have changed over the generations since it was made, we often ignore the difficulty and attach recent meanings to old pictures when we want to talk about the past.

If we do not push present people's explanations back through the history of their societies; that is, if we do not use 'ethnographic analogy' to explain the past, we can explain it in a different way, using the patterns formed by what people made and did. This chapter is about the start that has been made on that way of seeing the past, using patterns formed by the where, when and how of rock art in Australia. The rest of the book brings Aboriginal peoples' recent meanings to pictures on rock whenever possible and these are not intended to say anything about the past. When ideas about style are discussed, the ideas are those of outsiders who are using patterned information to try to explain history.

Australian rock art — paintings, engravings, drawings and stencils — is all physical information about history and most of it falls into the long period of Australia's prehistory. It can be formed into patterns — classified — to suggest explanations about itself and links with other kinds of patterned archaeological evidence. Archaeology is quite good at finding out about some things: what the climate was like, what people ate, how they got their food, and other material aspects of their lives such as tools, techniques, seasonal movements and trade routes.

Fire is a tool. Its remains, charcoal, allow

dates to be established, within certain limits, for the time it was burning. Other material occurring in the same archaeological layer as hearth remains is dated by them. Charcoal is necessary to date events by the carbon-14 method. It also helps greatly if people ate shellfish because shells create a preserving environment for the charcoal and other things. But evidence that is not associated with fire is more difficult to date. Such things as ochre mines, flint mines and stone tools not associated with camping places usually present this difficulty, as do engravings or paintings on rock faces.

To start a pattern for rock art, styles are distinguished from one another. Style is a picture's material expression; it can be used to say what particular kinds of pictures look like and how they differ from other kinds. This is difficult because people see different factors coming together to make one picture similar or different from another: size, form, materials, tools, technique, colour and decoration. Some classifications of style have included function — what the picture represents or means. We can only know this for some pictures and then only for the present. No matter how much a prehistoric picture reminds us of a lizard, a man or an evil spirit, we cannot, using our present modes of understanding at least, assume that our guess and the artist's intention match up. We can assume, though, that the artist depicted what he intended to depict and John Clegg, in particular, has spent time devising ways to arrive at prehistory by analysing pictures in a number of statistical ways. His concern with seeing what methods seem to produce useful answers before worrying about the philosophical problem of whether a label such as 'lizard' would ever be right reminds us that many descriptions of rock art should be taken with a grain of salt. The classifications of style in rock art that are most useful for prehistory are those based on form and technique.

Once styles have been separated they can be distributed in space: the places where they occur can be plotted on a map. The way such a distribution fits in with the distribution of other kinds of archaeological evidence can comment on the usefulness of the classification of styles. But we have records of only part of the many different kinds of evidence, and this makes usefulness harder to gauge.

Finding out when pictures were made is difficult. Mostly the superimposition of pictures of one style on pictures of another is the only way of plotting styles through time. This gives relative dating — style A comes before style B —

but does not say exactly when any style was practised. Deciding which picture was made on top of another is also much harder than it seems after perhaps thousands of years have worked to change the appearance of rock surfaces through erosion and patination. When relative dates for the styles in a rock art classification are worked out and tied in with where the styles occur, a pattern is formed which should fit with other archaeological patterns. Some of these patterns are based on larger amounts of recorded evidence and on more and better methods of getting answers, such as carbon-14 dating. What are thought to be the most useful of these answers will have been borne in mind in classifying rock art. Patterns in Australia's prehistory have been formed quite quickly in the short time since the study began. Often answers suggested by these patterns to questions of who, when, what and how have been shown to be wrong by new evidence. This has sometimes suggested different ways of looking at evidence and has led to fresh patterns being drawn.

The present framework of prehistory provides information which spans more than 40 000 years of the human occupation of Australia. It indicates that the first people to arrive in the country came from the northwest. This would have been easiest at a time when sea levels were very low, making water crossings fewer and shorter. Around 50 000 years ago and again about 20 000 years ago, vast amounts of the earth's water was locked in ice at the poles. At these times sea levels were very low and large areas of land emerged from the sea to enlarge land masses and join some now separate lands together. New Guinea and Tasmania were joined to the Australian mainland during those times. People could have come to what is now called Australia more easily during these two ice ages than they could at other times. There were a number of possible routes from Asia. Which or how many of them were used, to what extent people came deliberately or by accident, and what kind of water craft they used is not known. Most likely people arrived in Australia during both ice ages and even at other times. But we have evidence that people were already living in the southeast of the country more than 30 000 years ago and so the first people probably arrived during the earlier period of low sea levels.

The earliest widely available evidence of peoples' lives in Australia comes from the shores of a large freshwater lake, now dry and called Lake Mungo, in the west of what is now the State of New South Wales. The alkaline soils of the lake shore have preserved traces of charcoal from fire-places and carbon-14 dates show that they are more than 30 000 years old. Food remains from that time have provided a list of what people ate and stone tools have given clues about how they caught and collected food. A grave containing the skeleton of a man whose bones had been covered with ochre which had been brought some distance to the lake suggests that a ceremony had accompanied his burial. It shows that ochre was used as long ago as other things that are a part of peoples' lives.

No way has been found to tell how long an engraved or painted design has been on a rock. Engravings are likely to last longer than paintings but a great deal depends on the position and type of rock. In the open, the ochre used to make a painting fades and disappears quickly. If the rock is porous and allows the ochre to sink in, it will take longer for the marks to erode in the rain and wind. Erosion of rock surfaces removes signs of engraving too, and, all things being equal, the deeper the engraving the longer it will withstand these forces. The degree of patination on rock art is subject to too many variables to give a date — at least, until a great deal more work has been done on the subject. Most of the rock art archaeologists have been concerned with has been done in shelters, usually rock overhangs or wide, shallow caves. Here the pictures tend to be more protected from the elements, and the degree to which they are protected can be better understood for individual locations. Still, the idea that a painting *could* have been preserved on a rock wall for many thousands of years will not reveal how long it has actually been there unless, by some accident, part of it becomes involved in layers of earth which can be dated. No examples of art using more permanent materials, no decorated objects or sculptures of stone, clay or bone, have yet been excavated in Australia. These would help in dating and building up sequences of styles as they have in the study of Europe's Late Palaeolithic cave art.

The earliest Aboriginal drawings known to us at present are at Koonalda Cave, a sink-hole deep in the Nullarbor Plain. There, closely massed patterns of parallel grooves meander down in total darkness on the soft limestone walls. They were most likely made by peoples' fingertips. Other sets of grooves, including an area of cross-hatched lines, had also been abraded on the walls. The place was a flint quarry; workers needed to carry flaming torches to find their way to the seams, in some parts through crawling-passages. At some time after the patterns had been drawn on the walls, a great rock-fall occurred which partly covered them. Later miners or visitors dropped the charred remains of their torches on top of the rubble. The torches' remains are dated to about 20 000 years ago. This makes the drawings nearly as old as European Palaeolithic art, which is interesting; but their usefulness for the prehistory of art is limited because their style is the only example of its kind known and it does not compare with other art styles.

Lesley Maynard's scheme for examining and learning from Australia's rock art is the most recent and best justified of the very few attempts made at a continent-wide framework for this aspect of prehistory. The pattern she suggests distributes styles in space and time as other patterns do. Sequences of styles through time — their relative dates — have been proposed by looking at evidence from the pictures themselves, such as superimposition, and at geographical distribution. How long styles lasted and their absolute dates cannot be known at present. More may be learned as other archaeological work is done and more dates are accumulated.

Plotting different classes of art on maps to show their geographical distribution has the potential, Maynard notes, for revealing patterns which suggest new hypotheses about the art: 'They might relate to possible diffusion routes into the continent, the sequence in which the different styles entered Australia or evolved within it, or correlations with geographical or cultural regions or with other archaeological distribution maps'. More information can change the shape of a pattern or invalidate parts of it, and this is a problem at present with rock art, as Maynard goes on to say. There are far more art sites in Australia, and in more widespread places, than the fully recorded material shows. The surveys of Robert Edwards, undertaken over many years in various parts of the country, alone confirm this. If all the recorded information on Australian rock art is studied, a general idea of what is where can be gained, but a detailed distribution study has not yet been started. The work of a number of people whose regional studies could contribute to a detailed Australia-wide study is considered in Maynard's scheme. Some of this work is included in the regional descriptions of rock paintings later in this book.

Maynard talks about rock art of all kinds, bringing engraved, painted and drawn pictures into her broad pattern. There are some kinds of pictures in some areas that cannot be tied to the other styles or groups of styles that she pro-

After Maynard, in Mead, S. M., *Exploring the Visual Art of Oceania*, The University Press of Hawaii, p.98

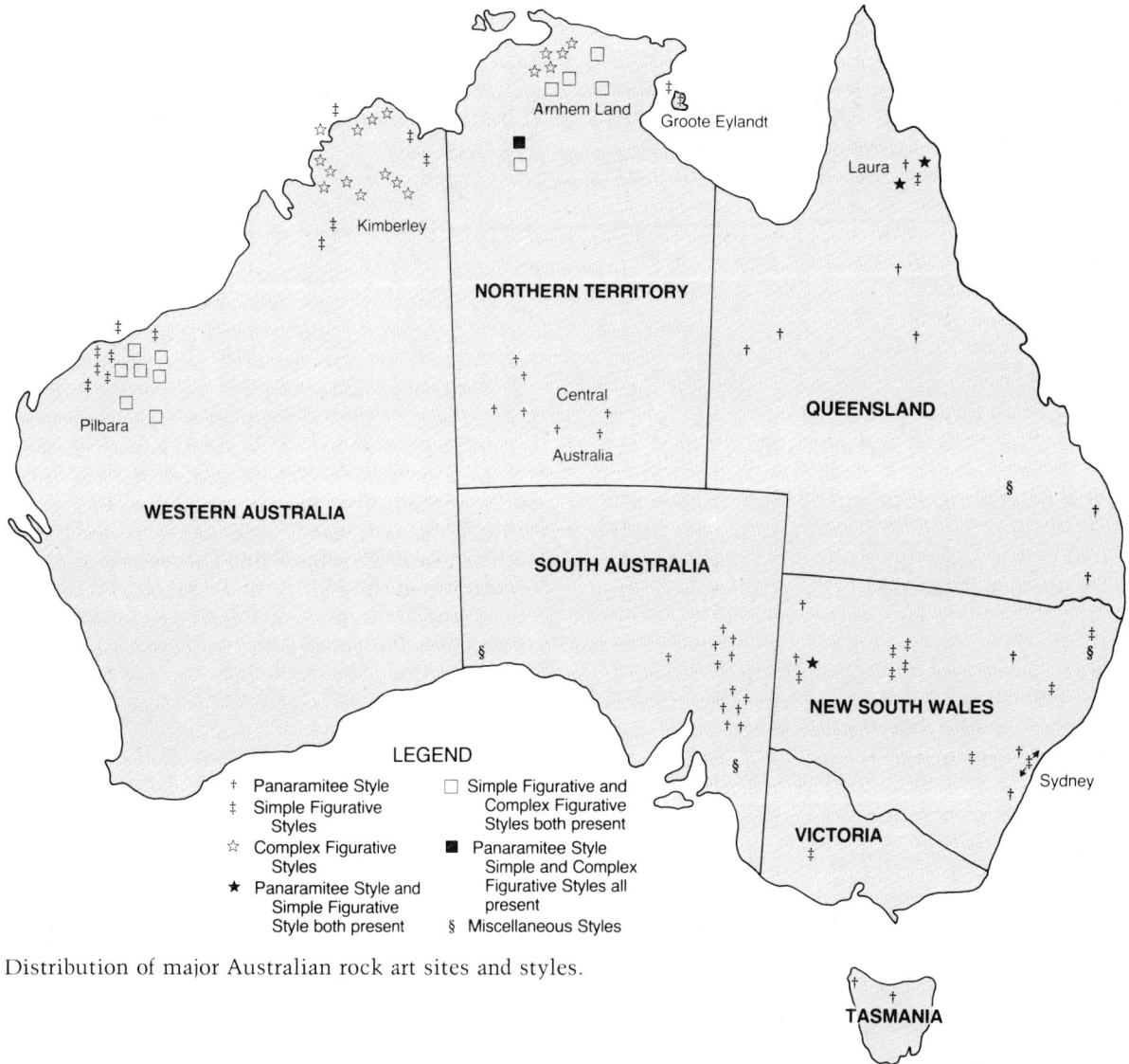

Arnhem Land

Groote Eylandt

Laura

Kimberley

NORTHERN TERRITORY

Central

Australia

Pilbara

QUEENSLAND

WESTERN AUSTRALIA

SOUTH AUSTRALIA

NEW SOUTH WALES

Sydney

VICTORIA

LEGEND

| | | | |
|---|---|---|---|
| † | Panaramitee Style | ☐ | Simple Figurative and Complex Figurative Styles both present |
| ‡ | Simple Figurative Styles | | |
| ☆ | Complex Figurative Styles | ■ | Panaramitee Style Simple and Complex Figurative Styles all present |
| ★ | Panaramitee Style and Simple Figurative Style both present | § | Miscellaneous Styles |

Distribution of major Australian rock art sites and styles.

TASMANIA

poses. The drawings in Koonalda Cave are one example. These must remain outside the system into which most rock art has been fitted for the time being, at least. Stencils, on the other hand, are found in every part of Australia in association with every body of cave paintings and drawings. Apparently they were made from very early rock art prehistory through to contact times when the range of subjects stencilled, hands, feet, utensils, small animals, expanded to include steel axes and other European artefacts. Being practised in so many places at so many times, stencils are not useful for classification at present.

The model is offered by Maynard as a way of seeing the prehistory of Australian rock art. It seems, as she notes, to fit what known facts are available but should not yet be used to explain other facts. This should wait until a completed structure has been built on this model, its successors or alternatives. This, briefly, is Maynard's view.

Based on factors of technique, form, motif, size and character, most of Australia's known rock art has been assigned to one of three major styles, or groups of styles. Paintings and engravings are separated only at the level of technique, painting being described as an additive process, engraving as a subtractive process. All factors are measurable and meaning of the kind that might have been explained by an artist is not included. Dimensions of time and space added to the style pattern shows that the earliest style practised was what Maynard has chosen to call the Panaramitee style.

Panaramitee style, named after a typical site in the southeast of South Australia, is an individual style not a grouping of styles as the two later phases are. It contains pecked engravings (probably made by indirect percussion rather than pounded directly out of the rock face with a smaller rock or stone) which are composed of bands and solid forms. There is a fairly small range of motifs and figures are usually not more than ten centimetres long. What appear to be bird and animal tracks are most common and there are a very few figures that remind people of animals — mostly lizards. (Labels such as 'tracks' or 'lizards' are only to make description easier: motifs can be measured and classed as 'A' or 'B' which is more valid but less interesting.) Non-figurative — geometrical — motifs include circles, which are very common and often presented as perfect concentric circles, crescents, groups of dots, radiating lines and line mazes known as 'tectiforms'. The relative proportion of the various kinds of motif remains consistent at all the sites which are included in the main area of Panaramitee style. Besides the sites in South Australia, another group of sites about a thousand kilometres away in Central Australia contains the same sorts of pecked pictures with almost identical relative proportions of kinds of motif.

Edwards did the groundwork on this style and also presented a case for its antiquity. This is based on a number of factors including comparative rates of arid-zone patination of rock surfaces, and the disintegration of engraved rock and the apparently complete erosion of pieces which had fallen from them in some places. In areas of Central Australia where Panaramitee style engravings are found, present and recent Aboriginals incorporate the engravings in their creation knowledge but say they did not make them. The engravings they do make are pounded, not pecked. Near the pecked engravings, other archaeological evidence has been found which often includes stone tools of kinds which are usually part of early assemblages — more than four thousand years old. At Ingaladdi near Katherine in the Northern Territory, an excavation by Mulvaney at the base of a thickly engraved sandstone outcrop disclosed pieces of sandstone which had fallen from the wall and been covered by later debris. The pieces had pecked engravings of tracks (apparently emu and kangaroo) and abraded grooves as had the rock face from which they had fallen. Carbon-14 dating of the layers of material at the site indicates that the engraved pieces fell from the wall between 7000 and 5000 years ago. We cannot tell how long before that they were made. In Tasmania, the engraved motifs are similar to Panaramitee style and this may say that the style had spread south before Tasmania was cut off from the mainland by rising seas about 10 000 years ago. Some of this evidence is stronger than other parts of it, but Maynard concludes that the style itself is more than 7000 years old, though not all examples need be so old. New evidence could confirm or change this view. Maynard's map shows the present distribution of the three styles.

Panaramitee style is broadly defined by its kinds of pecked motifs composed of bands and solid areas. It occurs at other places in the eastern half of the continent, but the relative proportions of motifs at the classic southern and central sites do not extend to the other known sites, and their age cannot be inferred from evidence relating to the classic sites. The style is defined by engravings and there are no engravings shown in this book. Probably no rock paintings still visible could match Panaramitee style engravings for age, but some echo the track and geometrical motifs. This can be seen in some of the plates of Central Australia and Flinders Ranges paintings (Plates 19-23).

The Simple Figurative styles form the next major rock art phase. A number of styles from widespread sites come together in this phase because they share comon features of motif and character. Technique may be different (unlike Panaramitee) and so both engraved and painted pictures may be included as Simple Figurative. Figures are characterised as consisting of a simplified, standardised silhouette, in outline or solid form, of a human or animal model. Decoration, when it occurs, is relatively simple, consisting of second-colour outline or of infills of stripes and dots. Where figures of this kind dominate regional styles, the styles belong in the Simple Figurative group. The engravings of the Sydney-Hawkesbury region are a good example of a style which falls into the Simple Figurative group. None is shown here, but some of the paintings of the Laura area of Cape York, another good example, are shown in Plates 29-37, and some from the Cobar district of New South Wales appear in Plates 25-27. The map shows the very wide distribution of Simple Figurative styles: it has been possible to include only a few examples of them in this book. This deficiency is slightly less marked in the case of the Complex Figurative styles.

Complex Figurative styles include some of those described at greatest length here: the Mimi and X-ray painting styles of Arnhem Land, and Bradshaw and Wandjina styles of Kimberley. The pounded engraving style found at some sites in the Pilbara is the other style included in Complex Figurative. The common characteristic of this group of styles consists in a degree of sophistication (or 'stylisation' or 'schematisation') greater than that shown in Simple Figurative styles. This may be expressed through the depiction of action, elegant and highly decorative features and ornaments, and delicate linework used to portray features including internal anatomy. Sexual themes are common and explicit in Complex Figurative styles.

These more sophisticated styles are the most recent styles where they occur, in the northwest quadrant of the continent. X-ray and Wandjina styles include pictures of recent subjects: Macassan praus, Dutch smoking pipes and English sailing ships as well as clothed foreigners, horses, cattle and guns (Plate 36). These styles superseded Mimi and Bradshaw styles in their respective regions. On the east coast of Australia no Complex Figurative styles are found and Simple Figurative is the most recent. This also depicts contact subjects. In Central and South Australia, the Panaramitee style is remote in time. The recent art of the Centre — rock painting and pounded engraving (showing recent European subjects), ground art and engraved sacred objects — mostly uses geometrical motifs similar to Panaramitee motifs. There are still very few figurative motifs used, but form, technique and relative proportion of motifs are different and so the recent art does not, in Maynard's terms, extend Panaramitee style into recent times, although it points to some continuity in the region's art history.

Extracting a wide view from her model, Maynard proposes a sequence of events in the prehistory of Australian rock art. More than ten thousand years ago people in most of the continent (which then included Tasmania) made rock engravings by the pecking technique in a small range of non-figurative and 'track' motifs. In a large area of Central and South Australia, some factor operated to keep the relative proportions of different motifs constant at each site. Further afield, in Queensland and Tasmania, these proportions were not maintained although range of motifs and their technique, form and size were identical. This widespread phase probably persisted for a very long time although it may not have been practised at the same time in each place, perhaps dying in one area while still spreading to another. At some stage, people in the Centre stopped making pecked engravings although some of the pictures themselves are still part of local creation knowledge. They now use similar motifs in rock paintings and poundings, ground art and on sacred objects. These kinds of art may have been made at the same time as, or before, the pecked engravings but we have no evidence. Around the northwest, north and east of the continent, the Panaramitee style was replaced, at an unknown time, by Simple Figurative styles. This naturalistic manner of depicting things may have spread from some point around the coast and into inland New South Wales and was probably a gradual process in any place since all Simple Figurative styles retain small numbers of non-figurative motifs. On the east coast, in Groote Eylandt, in western New South Wales and probably in parts of the Pilbara, Simple Figurative styles persisted until the present. But in the northwest of the continent these styles were replaced by a variety of Complex Figurative styles at some time long enough ago to allow for style changes.

Maynard's pattern and the view of history suggested by it are the results of years of work in a vast subject which is as yet incompletely recorded. Abbreviating a part of her work to illustrate a useful and valid way of looking at prehistory can only be unfair if not quite wrong. Some of her published work is listed in the bibliography with that of some other prehistorians. The subject is very interesting.

It will be clear now that the rock paintings shown here represent only a fragment of the styles, places and times in an enormous subject the full extent of which is not yet known. But these pictures give a general impression of (perhaps an introduction to) the great diversity of rock paintings in Australia, and the words tell how they can speak in different voices carrying different kinds of meaning. The present voice still speaks about conscious meanings and we can sometimes listen although the evidence of our continuing ignorance suggests we seldom bother. The voice of the past is made to speak its different kinds of meaning to outsiders through patterned remains. This foreign exploration of their ancient knowledge in pursuit of a global history of humankind may cause fleeting amusement to Aboriginal people, especially when new scientific wisdom agrees with their oral wisdom about rising sea levels, erupting volcanoes and giant animals. This has surprised everyone except the people themselves, but any satisfaction or amusement derived by them from the situation has been clad in the heaviest, most bitter irony.

# 2
# LISTENING TO PEOPLE: DREAMINGS

Mowaljarlai, elder of the Ngarinyin people, tells of Wandjina at Wanalirri shelter, Kimberley.

In the beginning (so the Gunwinggu children are taught) the earth was dark always and peopled by beings who waited, watched, travelled and did things which made the earth the way it is now. One of these beings was the sun woman who lived buried in the depths of the world through long ages, knowing that her terrible light and heat would destroy all things on the face of the earth. She gave birth to a daughter, a tiny radiant being who, when she grew older, would be able to look on the earth and give light to the people without burning them to ashes. The sun lives still at the burning centre of the world, and each morning she lifts her daughter to the eastern sky to light the days of her kinspeople as they find food and grow in their care and knowledge of the way.

This is how some parts of the great knowledge of the beginnings of all things look when they have been written down in a foreign language. English is not a tongue used to teach about the beginnings of any peoples except at second hand, though it may prove brilliantly adapted to foretell the end of all things.

In that great, dark waiting time at all peoples' beginning (so Karraru people all understand) their father went to a deep cave beneath the plain at the southern end of the land. There he carefully woke the beautiful sun mother who slept at the centre of the earth's darkness. Light danced from her opening eyes, bouncing from the surface of the land and making it visible for the creatures who would soon have eyes to see it. The sun mother travelled over the land, bathing it in warmth and light and coaxing into life leafy bushes, trees and waving grasses. Insects whirred and crept over the land in company with the snakes and lizards, while the birds took wing and saw the wakening movements of more and more of the earth's creatures as they stirred at the sun mother's gentle touch. The sun mother taught them all the way of henceforward, explaining the pattern she had designed for the seasons. When these things had been well taught, she showed all creatures how she had planned that they should have a time of rest in each day, for she sank down beneath the earth at the west of the land, relieving their anxious wait by rising the next morning in the eastern sky as she has done always from that time forward.

The things of nature and the things of culture (so all people are taught) were created and born together of the powers who were there at the beginning of the world. They are here still, but have taken themselves from the sight of almost all people since they have completed their early task of turning time, space and life into knowledge. There are many powers. They are not the same as ordinary people since they can do extraordinary things including shaping the world and the people, animals and plants in it. Yet they are related to the people in the same sorts of ways in which the people are related to each other. They are like people and they are like other creatures, yet such is their power to change and direct that they appear, in word and picture, as one, the other, or both. The powers communicate their presence to the people through all natural things and living creatures which are symbols of themselves, and through the people themselves by creating in them the power to express knowledge through songs, ceremonies and pictures.

When the world was young (so the Kakadu have always known) spirit children were brought across the water in the great body of an all-powerful being. Imberombera travelled about the country, her body ploughing out river valleys and throwing up hills, and put down in the new places yams and other plants that she had brought in the dilly-bags hanging on her head. She left children, too, in the various places after teaching them the different languages they were to speak. This first mother made her children creative and productive; they used their languages to instruct their own children in all the detail of custom and law, country and creature, and of the mother-being herself and the signs by which she reminded the people of her presence.

Some creative beings arose to work and teach in the country they shaped for one group of people and, when it was done, went into the earth there, belonging forever in special, regional knowledge. But the people who relate that knowledge in stories have many other stories which tell of the travels of creator-ancestors who came from other places and stayed, or went on from their country to end their journey somewhere else. In all places the land is the enduring symbol of the power which gave life to it. The people, being a special part of this creation, hold the land and its creatures in trust for the great beings on their instructions, and cannot leave it, give it to others or allow its injury except at the peril of their existence. Those who lose their dreaming are themselves lost; cut adrift from their spiritual roots and able to exist only in flesh and blood. When this dies, nothing of it survives and the cultural point of existence is wiped away.

This understanding of the importance of religion — dreaming — for the continuing existence of Aboriginal cultures emerges from what outsiders have been told and have been able to grasp of it. It is given to outsiders usually as it is given to Aboriginal children — as stories which explain how things came to be the way they are. But elder men and elder women hold knowledge about why things are, and this knowledge is expressed in ritual with songs, dances, objects and designs, some of which men and women hold secret from each other and from outsiders. Some high knowledge is shared among all elder people, in different ways and degrees in different groups, and some of it has been told to outsiders.

What outsiders have said and written about the dreaming results from what they thought they heard and how they were able to make sense of it. Since Captain Cook's day, many European foreigners have been accepted as not-enemies, as friends and as kin in many groups all over Australia. Some of these outsiders, who have been serious for whatever reason in their bid for acceptance by the people, have learned the language of particular groups. Some have come to speak it fluently, have stood as kin to all members of the group and have had knowledge of many degrees passed to them. Some believe they have had knowledge of the highest degree given to them in absolute trust forever, or against the loss of their dreaming by the group. Some have even broken this trust.

Whatever has been handed on by these outsiders to others has been translated, in word and idea, so that it could be spoken and thought about in another culture. There are many who insist that information of high kinds does not survive this process. And the stories which are told to children are probably simplified versions of parts of great knowledge which contain the seeds, or the clues to, the knowledge itself.

Many people have made it their business to try to explain to other cultures what they believe they understand of particular Aboriginal cultures — from economic systems to social structures to religious philosophy. They have had to interpret the information they have been given, either by the people through stories or their explantions or through the material remains of their long-dead ancestors. These interpretations are often passed on as if they were fact, as if they represented the truth. Dampier announced, from what he saw and heard of Aboriginals, that they represented the most miserable form of human life. Others agreed, at first and second hand. R. M. Berndt, more recently and among many others, believes they are the representatives of intensely satisfying cultures of great complexity and sophistica-

tion which they carry with dignity and genius. While Berndt's experience and intellectual breadth make his view infinitely more acceptable than Dampier's, both views are still interpretations.

Cautiously generalising, then, it can be said that a few creator-powers were thought of as single beings in human form who stood as original mothers or fathers to all people. If they were few, it was probably because the concept sat uneasily in the kinship network. If a being was father to any person, he could not also be father to that person's wife or husband. Because they cannot be incorporated in the real system of relationships between groups and individuals, they have been classified anthropologically as transcendental powers — that is, they transcend the important part of the social order which is kinship.

Imberombera, who brought the Kakadu people and other peoples of Arnhem Land across the water as spirit children may be such an all-mother. Mutjingga is all-mother for the Murin-batha, but she is not always thought of or shown in pictures as wholly human in form. She may be seen partly in snake form. It is told that she swallowed some children who had been left in her care and was pursued by the people who discovered what she had done. They caught up with her, speared her and opened her belly, pulling the missing children from her womb. The children were washed and then dried in smoke from the fire, painted with ochre and adorned with possum hair bands. These things were the signs of initiation and, wearing them, the children were returned to their rejoicing mothers at camp.

Like the peoples with all-mothers, those with an all-father made strong connections between the creator-power and the initiation of youth in the stage-by-stage acquisition of wisdom. For different groups he had different names, but in essence he had human form and had ascended to the sky from where he took an all-seeing interest in the people and particularly their conduct of male initiation. The initiation rites he decreed and supervised mostly took place in the south of Australia, and they are no longer (or, at least, not at present) practised. Many of the descendants of those elders who, before the turn of the last century and afterwards, told R. H. Mathews and A. W. Howitt the names, powers and activities of their all-father, have lost their dreaming.

For the Theddora people, Daramulun was all-father and the women, at least, believed that he came down with a noise like thunder to make boys into men. Women and children of the Wiradthuri believed that Dhuramoolan was sent by Baiamai, the all-father, to initiate boys by destroying them, moulding their ashes again into human form, but each missing a tooth, and restoring them to life and their poeple. The missing tooth was an outward sign that this task had been accomplished. Wiradthuri men, however, knew something that the women did not know, and they kept the secret from the women although they entrusted it to Mathews. This is an account of the story.

Baiamai entrusted the initiation of the boys to Dhuramoolan, but Dhuramoolan deceived the all-father. He would take the boys away and, instead of destroying and remaking them each without a tooth, he would kill and eat a few and send the others back after pulling out a tooth from each one. Dhuramoolan explained to Baiamai that the missing boys had fallen ill and died, but the all-father's suspicions grew and he questioned the terrified survivors until they told him the truth. Baiamai's anger was great, and he destroyed Dhuramoolan, leaving only his awful voice in the trees. It could be heard when a wooden bullroarer was swung. Baiami then gave instructions to the Wiradthuri elders. They would from that time onwards initiate the boys themselves, swinging a bullroarer to imitate Dhuramoolan's voice, but they would keep this secret from the women and children who should continue to believe that the boys were destroyed and restored to life by Dhuramoolan. The instructions had been obeyed ever since, with elaborate preparations and dramatic scenes designed to reinforce the mothers' belief that Dhuramoolan had indeed come with terrifying sounds and sensations as they lay with their faces in the earth to carry off their sons. The boys themselves were enlightened at a crucial moment during the initiation rite and sworn to secrecy on pain of death.

The initiation of Murimbata boys in fear of their all-mother takes place according to a similar deception, and these accounts have fascinated anthropologists and others for a number of reasons as they attempted to piece together their interpretations of the relations between Aboriginals and their creator-powers. Not least fascinating was an attempt to understand the exclusion of women from enlightenment according to religious law. This was something the investigators felt especially able to deal with since most of them came from Christian societies which also taught the mystification and exclusion of women. Other stories show how present men explain, through the symbols of the powers that they deal with now, the social role of women in their groups.

There are few powers who stand as the mother or father of all people, but many who have special relationships with particular sections of groups and are easily incorporated in the kinship system. These have been called 'totemic powers', but the pitfalls of putting creators — or stone tools — in foreign filing systems are seen when some powers refuse to fall neatly into place. What is usually called the Rainbow Serpent, for want of a better translation, sometimes seems to outsiders so similar to an all-mother that it is hard to see where one leaves off and the other begins. This problem is real only to the filing clerks and has been answered to the satisfaction of some of them at least, by seeing the Rainbow Serpent as a bridge between the transcendental and the totemic powers. This also has the advantage of being a poetical image.

When Thuwathu, the rainbow serpent, came up from the south (as the Larumbanda of Mornington Island know) he had with him his sister, Bulthugu the rock-cod, and her baby daughter Gindidbu the willy-wagtail. Thuwathu made camp at Jalga-Gindidbu. He and his companions, the spotted stingray, the bluefish, the trevally, the bone fish, the seagull Garngurr and the bee, goanna, wallaby, turtle, dugong, shark and others, built their shelters there with Thuwathu's big place in the centre. The rock-cod woman and her willy-wagtail daughter had no shelter. One evening a great storm broke over Jalga-Gindidbu and, as the rain became heavier, Bulthugu feared that her baby would become cold and fall ill. She called to Thuwathu, her brother, asleep in his snug shelter, to find room for the little willy-wagtail. Thuwathu was tired and grumbled at his sister, telling her that there was no room — she should go away and not disturb him. As soon as the mother spied a place to tuck her daughter in the safety of his shelter, Thuwathu moved some part of his great body into that nook and told her to go away. Bulthugu stoked her fire and wrapped her baby in bark beside it, watching the child and pleading with her brother by turns. Soon, after Thuwathu had shifted himself about, taking up this corner with hig huge knees, that with his great horns and the other with his long penis, the baby began to shiver and became ill. The mother began to cry for her child and, when the little willy-wagtail died, she cut her head and her arms in her grief.

Bulthugu's anger at her brother was very great. She tied and lit a bark torch and set fire with it all around Thuwathu's shelter. He cried out in pain, cursing his sister, and rolled out of the flames, burning and suffering. Crawling away with his colours all burnt, he sang a terrible song, his great jaws ploughing up the earth as he went. The water followed Thuwathu as he gouged out the earth in his path, and his burning body fired the country all about. The sea came in to put out the fire, leaving that place of the willy-wagtail, Jalga-Gindidbu, underneath it to this day. He travelled on, suffering and ill, making the great river in his wake, singing and vomiting up new life to fill the country. Trevally and mud crabs, sugar-bag bees, swamp turtle and water-lilies, goanna, wallaby and bloodwood trees were left in their places. Ribs fell from his burnt and blistered body and, where they fell, the gidyea boomerang trees grew. Where his blood spread over the salt-pan red ochre is now found. Thuwathu's own people, the rainbows, sang in sorrow when he came to them so thin and ill, and cut themselves with sharp stones as they mourned. The old man died at Bugargun on his way back to his country, fretting over his sister and her child. A great spring came up there and Thuwathu went down into its waters, but his spirit lives still in every well and waterhole, and his eye follows the world in each shooting star. Until this day, the young men see the dances and hear the songs of Thuwathu's story at their initiation as they learn the laws of their people. Especially they learn the importance of their responsibility for their sisters' children.

Paintings and engravings on large rock surfaces, on smaller, special rocks or on wood and bark show the ancestor spirits and powers in naturalistic or symbolic form. Painted designs on the bodies of people involved in all kinds of ceremonies, from secret to full community occasions, and the ornamentation worn, also represent aspects of the beings whose works, travels and teachings are being celebrated. Even the greatest creators and teachers can have good and evil aspects. They often behave, or behaved, in ways extremely human and frail. The good teachings are followed and the wrong actions are sometimes used as examples of what people ought not to do.

Gidegal the moon (as the Larumbanda know) gave the people the law to follow in the initiation of boys in men's wisdom. He also left the Jarrada song-cycle and the sacred ceremony through which men can sing women to them as wives or lovers. The ground designs, decorated objects, body paint and ritual are elaborate and carefully made — and the Jarrada songs of Gidegal never fail. Gidegal himself, when he was on the earth, was a renowned lover of women and used his songs to great effect, and not always in a proper way. His people still succumb, from time to time, to the temptation of using the songs to secure the affections of other men's wives.

Gidegal was greedy and selfish, too. One day, while he was on the earth and not long after he had made the first initiation ceremony, he heard the people, who had changed into birds, animals, fishes and other creatures, holding a great dance ceremony. He went to them and, standing by their fire, he instructed them to dance harder. Soon they were dancing so well and energetically that they could not see each other for the dust that rose from their pounding feet. Gidegal had spied a dugong cooking in the fire and, under cover of the dust, he ate some and stole the rest, making off with it as fast as he could run. A woman gave the alarm and the men pursued Gidegal and, when they eventually caught him, they struck him with their stone axes and spears until he was dead. The men cut Gidegal into four pieces and threw them into the sky where they remained. Gidegal came back to life, up there in the sky. At first he appeared in the west, just after sunset, lying on his back like a baby in a bark cradle. Then he grew fatter, his stomach rounding out as if with dugong meat, and afterwards he faded slowly until he was like a thin stooped old man. He has been dying and returning to life like this ever since and, when he is in eclipse, you can see the red blood from the wounds he suffered on the earth.

Giridin the moon man (as the Nygina people have long known) came down from his lonely place in the sky one day to find a woman to love. He pretended to the people that he needed a guide through their country that night and they, knowing that the moon must travel at night, were pleased to help and offered him a young boy as a guide. Giridin refused, making the excuse that the boy might play with the special initiates' bone ornament in his nose and be distracted. The Moon refused all the peoples' offers of boys at the various stages of knowledge, making similar excuses and saying they were not suitable. The men began to show impatience after Giridin had refused girls of various ages and rashly offered him a guide from amongst the young women at the secret camp. Well pleased, the crafty Moon made haste to the women's camp where he could now go without hindrance. After making himself attractive to the women in voice and appearance and making love-play with them as they gathered some fruit he had shown them, he chose one earth maiden, Moorlamuda, and lay with her and loved her all night. In the morning, a baby was born, and Giridin slept so long that he had to hurry back to his place in the sky as the sun was lighting the land. Sometimes, when there has been no moon in the sky at night, he can be seen the next day, hurrying back home after spending the night with the earth women. Sometimes, too, Moorlamuda's baby can be seen cradled in the arms of the old moon.

A very long time ago (as a Tiwi child has told us) all the birds lived together near a big waterhole. Whistle Duck was the wife of Rainbow, who lived there with the birds. Rainbow was fat and handsome and had stolen Whistle Duck from Bat who was a wonderful dancer. Bat plotted to take his lawful wife back from Rainbow who was lazy and used to lie under a tree, keeping Whistle Duck close by his side. Bat spent a lot of time in his cave making spears so that he could kill Rainbow. He tested the spearpoints by cutting his nose or face with them, but they were never sharp enough to kill his rival. One day, Bat found and sharpened an excellent piece of stone and, when he tested it, it cut his nose and some of his face right off, leaving him looking the way bats do today. Hiding his new spear in the bushes, Bat joined in a big dance festival the birds were holding at the camp. Bat's wonderful dancing was admired by everyone but Rainbow, who lay under a tree with Whistle Duck beside him. When everyone had gone to sleep, Bat crept out to fetch his spear and threw it with all his might at the sleeping Rainbow. With a great scream, Rainbow thrashed about on the ground as the birds flew away in terror. Whistle Duck and Bat saw Rainbow roll into a waterhole where he stays even now. When it rains he often arches up from the waterhole and stretches his body across the sky, and you can still see the bright blood flowing down it.

All over Australia the stories, great and small, are told to the proper people at the proper time. The paths of the creator-powers link up the places where their mighty deeds took place and where other powers left descendants of Wallaby, Emu, Goanna, Yam, and a host of others. Teachings are often followed, correct observance of ritual carries the religious law down through the generations, and only in old age can any person expect to have the great wisdom of dreaming, to receive the secret keys which unlock real understanding.

# 3
# PICTURES AND PEOPLE

Jagamurro, Ngarinyin elder, sings of *mayangarri* events at Dilangarri, Kimberley.

## Life and Learning

In Aboriginal societies individually and as a whole, there exists a great force — a religious force — which binds all aspects of life and death in a continuing tradition which outsiders find hard to understand. It is expressed in plans for living which have proved successful for a long time. Many changes have occurred, and those that have passed into tradition have probably made it easier or more pleasant to put the life schemes into operation. Life is full of what people feel about their world: pleasure in entertainment, grief for dead friends, fear of evil forces and punishment, satisfaction from tasks well done and from lessons well taught and learned. Visual arts of many kinds express the things that people believe in and respond to in everyday life or on particular, significant occasions.

No one person can carry the complete learning of a society, but by the time an Aboriginal man is old, he can expect to know most of the huge body of information carried in his own society. He will have all the knowledge he inherits directly from the creation, and this knowledge, pooled with that kept by the other old men, forms the complete wisdom of the group. He may be specialised in certain forms of knowledge, as others are, and he will pass on his knowledge at the proper time to those who properly inherit it.

In teaching and learning, in ritual, celebration and play, pictures and symbols are painted, drawn, engraved, carved and constructed in a huge variety of ways to extend the images of the vast body of knowledge carried in the spoken word. Like the points of knowledge, their visual representations have descended, changing, through time. These pictures are still partly accessible to the outside eye. But they must be explained by the stories they represent if their particular meanings are to be understood.

Aboriginal religion binds the people, their land and the spirit powers in a great scheme that provides answers to all of life's questions. This means that religion ultimately embraces all of life and is expressed in work, play, song, dance, music and all the visual arts. There was always time for the telling of the stories, the performance of the rituals, and the making of the visual objects. It is hard to imagine where there could be room in the world to store all the art in all its forms that must have been created over all those thousands of years.

A great deal of art was transient — created and destroyed by the ceremony which inspired it.

The huge 'ground canvasses' of the deserts, drawn, sculpted and decorated on many square metres of earth, were pounded into oblivion by the feet of the dancers celebrating their significance. Many emblems painted on bark or constructed from wood, coloured thread, feathers, shells and stone were destroyed or abandoned at the conclusion of ceremonies. The designs painted on peoples' bodies or applied in feather-down or kapok over gum or blood wore off in the heat of the dance, and headdresses of feathers and circlets of fresh leaves on arms and legs relied on the wearer and the occasion for their form and significance. New art was created when and where the occasion demanded it. Articles of everyday life, such as carrying dishes, weapons and normal apparel and ornaments were decorated, and these went with the people as they followed the seasons and the dreaming routes. But they were eventually worn out, broken and replaced and were often made from perishable materials which cannot be traced for long after being discarded.

Baler shell and pearl shell ornaments are not so perishable. The shell is shaped and smoothed at its edges to form an oval or round pendant. Its surface is often engraved with a pattern which may have red ochre or charcoal rubbed into it so that it stands out sharply from its background. A hole at the top of the pendant allows it to be threaded on a string. Baler shells are found in coastal waters of Cape York and Kimberley and ornaments made from them have been found in the south of the country, having travelled through ceremonial exchange systems involving many groups. Pearl shell ornaments from Kimberley also moved widely. Often, when shells reached distant places, they acquired new significance in local ritual.

Wooden items, such as shields, decorated often with fine linear patterns, do not survive long after being thrown away. The possum skin cloaks of the south are even less likely to be found. Although early white settlers and explorers reported their use widely, only seven of them are known to exist now. Worn with the fur next to the wearer's skin, the outside was often decorated with patterns of scored lines or designs applied in ochre.

Pictures and designs painted with ochre, clay or charcoal on bark decay quickly. It is believed that people used to paint the inside of their bark shelters and, when they moved on, the shelters and their art eventually collapsed and decayed. Sheets of bark were painted for ritual use, too. From the south of the country, where people frequently painted on bark, only two examples survive in museums. Sir Baldwin Spencer recognised the significance of bark paintings and, around 1912, collected over 200 of them at Oenpelli in Arnhem Land. Artists of the north still paint their dreamings on bark, but the south has long been empty of this art form.

Great wooden carvings and sculptures, such as the Pukamani poles used in Tiwi mortuary rites, can see a number of generations come and go, but in the history of a land they exist only briefly. This is true, too, of carved trees which marked ceremonial or burial grounds, mostly in New South Wales. An area of bark was stripped from the trees and patterns of lines, often arranged in chevrons or curling in tendrils, were cut into the smooth wood. There are some still standing, usually with bark regrowth intruding on the carvings. They will not last, for fire is a constant danger and decay is inevitable.

The most enduring of the art forms is the painting and engraving of designs on rock. Even this is ephemeral in the face of long ages of exposure to the forces of nature. The designs can often be explained by people who can, and do, paint the same stories in the same way and for the same reasons, on bark or with other materials. These other, less enduring, objects permit a comparison of designs and styles, and in this way, too, rock art can be seen to belong with all the other forms of expression in the great scheme for living.

Art is used to explain things and to record their explanation. Flat boards and stones record the beliefs and explanations painted or engraved on them in various degrees of secrecy and at various levels of sacredness — often on the one object. A twig or finger drawn through the dust will explain a plan, a route or the appearance of something quicker and often better than words alone could do. Objects may be hidden away or displayed to exlain a host of beliefs to generations of people, and the dust designs may blow away or be trampled on. The pictures on rock may wait in the shadows of forbidden places to describe and teach sacred lessons to chosen students, or they may fade in the sun and smoke and activity of whole families as they explain aspects of everyday life or common religion. Still, their purpose is to carry knowledge whether their form and content inspire awe, admiration or more mundane thoughts and feelings.

Rules abound in Aboriginal societies, as in all others. One society's rules deal with particular aspects of life in ways that are often different from the way those things are dealt with in other societies. The societies divide their members into classes in systems which are governed by the rules of descent and marriage. All features and inhabitants of the natural world belong in the same systems as do all the powers of the supernatural world. Everything has its proper place in the world system for each society and this fact has led outside thinkers to ascribe a passion for order to the Aboriginal people. But the ways in which this order operates are extremely complicated, as any anthropological debate or treatise on Aboriginal kinship will demonstrate. A framework of classes for regulating people's activities probably acts as a prescription for proper behaviour rather than an account of what people actually do.

One important activity is marriage, and this is hedged about by rules which are not only complex but extremly restricting. No man should marry a woman belonging in the same class — all people 'marry out'. Within the permitted range, men are free to choose a wife on the basis of proper exchange. Women, being objects of such exchange, are not free to choose in any sense. They are bestowed. Freedom belongs to the rulers, but the rulers are not simply the male members of society, they are the older men. This group guards its authority against all other groups but, of them, boys and younger men can expect eventually to become members of the ruling group.

In guarding their authority, elders deny women the religious and social enlightenment which freedom would allow them. Boys are enlightened as their education progresses. Women have their own system of education leading to enlightenment, and some of this is kept secret from men. But it is said to operate on a smaller scale at a lower level, and the art which expresses it is supposed, likewise, to be less significant in society.

Art of all kinds, and particularly high religious art, is apparently very much a male preserve. Any museum or gallery catalogue of Aboriginal art will list little other than baskets, dishes, mats and ornaments under 'women's art' — beautiful and skilfully executed as they may be. By and large, men are the painters and sculptors of today, expressing in their art the great religious and social knowledge they keep for the society. If women had aimed to develop and expand the art, including the dance, song and drama, of their own ritual life, they would have been put into competition with men for the 'social time' to prepare and perform it. Given that 'passion for order' and the strength of tradition, it is no more likely that men would have yielded to such pressure than it is that women would have considered applying it.

Certain men are responsible for the designs, the making of ritual objects and body decoration for particular ceremonies. They are the keepers of the special knowledge being celebrated, and they teach the knowledge of its representation to their proper heirs. Women do the same in their own ceremonial life. Boys and girls learn to express themselves early. They are taught to make and recognise bird and animal tracks in the sand and are encouraged to draw the things they see around them in the same way. After initiation, all young men become artists — that sort of expression is part of the knowledge they receive and all must be able to pass it on in its artistic forms as well as in all the other ways. Naturally, some are more talented than others and they are recognised but not distinguished socially.

In the special learning process of initiation, boys are taken to sacred places which are often also secret places. Their sacredness is sometimes marked by art of one form or another, whether portable objects, stone or earth arrangements or rock pictures. This is used to illustrate the knowledge the boys are acquiring, but it is often the direct visual representation of the religious figure or power in whose service the knowledge is carried, and so all the correct attitudes, behaviour and ritual approaches must be taught at the same time.

In Kimberley, children are taken to some of the great Wandjina places. When they arrive at the border of the country where the Wandjina's influence is strongest, the adults warn the children not to break any branch or disturb any rock; they must not shuffle their feet, but must walk firmly. The teachers address the Wandjina and ask him not to be angry because they are disturbing him, but to be pleased that they are bringing children to learn from him.

The children know that the Wandjina is *mahmah*, special, pure and sacred. Children, too are *mahmah*, as are women. Men, once they have reached the stage of their initiation in which they have received most of the patterns of body scars, are no longer *mahmah* since they have become the servants of the Wandjina and all that is *mahmah* in their society. The children are warned not to make any careless movements, not to touch an image of the Wandjina or to disturb a pool of *wunggud* water, for all these things are wrong and will anger the Wandjina who would then send great winds, rain and hailstorms to destroy the people or would rise from the *wunggud* water as a snake to swallow

an intruder. The children see the images of the great mouthless Wandjina, the snake images and those of the other teachers as well as images of the spirit beings of folklore. At that time, they are taught the things they are able to understand and should learn.

A Ngarinyin elder says:

I took the children to the *wunggud* cave; I warned them, don't play around. This Wandjina is *mahmah*, don't touch him or he'll send rain. We carry this knowledge from our ancestors and it's important. You see all these snakes? These are *wunggud* snakes and Wandjina. If you touch he gets angry, sends wind and rain and destroys us. All the *jarra* [hailstones] come from the snake and destroy us. That's his power. I tell them each snake painting has a name — we count and show: this one is that woman, that one is that man.

I take the Mandangarri boy to the place. I say, this is your totem: you belong here. Don't think that because you own this you can do anything you like. You must listen to me and learn till you grow up. You will understand properly when you grow up — old man. You will take charge and tell other people and they will ask you.

Mandangarri is the saliva of the snake, often left as small rocks at *wunggud* places. The snakes previously had human form; some of them remained as people: 'People and spirits — but really the same thing — one clan. When Mandangarri die out, they are still there in the cave'.

The days of most people are not spent in philosophising about the meaning of life. Rather, they are spent in growing into the beliefs and behaviour of their societies, in soaking up and expressing those beliefs while their philosophers ponder and analyse the consistencies and contradictions contained in them. As Aboriginal philosophers ponder and come to new understandings of the way life is, adjustments may be made to everyday and ritual expressions which bring them in line with developments in thinking. From time to time, adjustments will be made to stories or to explanations of things. They may not at first, or even ever, replace older explanations, but may exist alongside them. The visual expressions of the ideas, in ritual or art, may also change, but not necessarily.

Ideas change in peoples' heads, but do people change them by just thinking and deciding? Aboriginal people often say that when they create and teach they are simply acting as agents for the spirit powers who, between them, created and taught everything that men know. But people behave politically; they constantly balance old values and new realities. In this sense, the dreaming is a constant force for change. Although the Australian dreaming, like all dreamings, was born in peoples' minds, rode down countless generations in them and continues to be creative, the people often accord all creative activity to the spirit powers. The Wandjinas painted themselves on the rock a long time ago; men merely renew the images. A new song was given to a man by the spirits only last year, and a healer gains his power through the *wunggud* snake in his stomach.

## The power of places

Northeast from King Sound where the King Leopold Range springs up from the grassy plain, past a place where ritual renews goanna spirits, you look to the east towards the country of the Warwa people where mighty Sandawarra strode underground to die, bloodied by countless bullets from the troopers' guns.

At the place where Iminji Wandjina rested and left behind the spring, the new moon lights the hills to the north where he painted himself on the rock. Glimmering across the sky, Lejmarro, the milky way, reflects the myriad points of Ngarinyin law as the stories are sung and it is told how the emu became impatient and, not waiting her turn with the other creatures, stole the special crushed berries from the spirit bowl. She ran with them across the sky and the land with the birds and animals crying close behind her, leaving her mark in the places where she paused.

As the country of Brr-Landad is left under the morning sun, Ngarinyin country is reached, at first stony *garawud* ground — basalt — where plants and animals feel unwelcome. At Banggi, the Wandjina said, 'I'm going up', and he climbed up and painted himself there in *memanggad* country where the sandstone provides plenty of food for all creatures.

To the north is the *garren* pillow place where Garren Wandjina stopped to rest. There on the horizon is Wadaburrgan, the crying place in the Wanggi hills where the little Waranga Wandjina came after running away. In all the places he stopped, he cried and sniffed and left white yams in the ground. He went on and painted himself at Dingan. The emu ran all along these Wanggi hills, carrying the berries she stole in the milky way.

Mowaljarlai cuts digging sticks from a *ngarwanji* bush, the same smooth, strong wood used for pressure-flaking elegant Wodoi spearpoints. As he trims the sticks he sings a dancing song about a beautiful woman whose laugh has the power to draw all men to her.

At Darranjingarri, a host of *jungari* Wandjina women stand, their roots anchored in the earth where the boab nuts fall from the branches crowning their great bottle-shaped trunks. A permanent spring fills the waterhole there. Its soft, sweet *memanggad* water is dappled with water lily pads and the berry trees and yams have settled all about that place where nobody is thirsty. One of the *jungari* boab women stands

Baobab trees, Kimberley.

closer than her sisters to the Darranjingarri snake water, but they all remember the time not long ago when they stood in terrible silence and watched their men die slowly on the scorching sandstone. They still hear the fading hoofbeats of the horses carrying away the police troopers and the bloody knives they used to cut the feet from the chained men.

We are as silent as the *jungari* women as the dust boils behind us. But the Bijili place is peaceful; the *bijili* are resting now, in the middle of the day, and we will be gone by dusk when they would swarm above the little creek, whining and stinging. Beside the snake creek, where it widens in a long pool, a cleared dancing space

32

rings an old tree. Here to Laji Nyoliyan, the witchetty grub spirit place, come the boys as they are being made into Ngarinyin men. Now it is quiet; Ngun the magpie goose returns and, climbing out of the water onto a boulder, stands gazing up the creek towards a place where a snake spirit is painted on the rock.

At Wah, Jilgi brings us roasted meat as we wait for Jagamurro to roll his swag. The emu only knows one master — and Jagamurro is inside, gathering his things. We scatter, putting the truck between us and the emu's one fierce black eye as he prances at us, making 'bonk-bonk, bonk-bonk' in his long throat. The old lady, Jagamurro's wife, shrieks and waves her stick at the flapping menace and he retires a little, sidling and ducking, as we continue our conversations.

Jagamurro the old doctor-man, with the power of the spirit snake in his stomach, wedged in with us among the swags in the open back of the little truck. We cool ourselves and wash off some of the dust in the creek where we arrive just before sunset. This is a special camp of Mowaljarlai's, and some Mowanjum people come there just as we do. Daisy Utemorrah is with them and, later, she tells us the story of

The Wandjina, Wojin, painted at Budbunjoningarri, Kimberley, with Dumbi the owl.

Dumbi the owl as we sit with the children around the campfire.

The young Dumbi was pulled from his nest by some boys long ago. They pulled out his feathers, maimed him with a stick and threw stones at him; they threw him into the air, laughing and jeering, 'Fly! Fly now if you can!' Dumbi fell back to the earth. The boys threw him up again and, to their amazement, he disappeared into the sky, for Dumbi was the son of a Wandjina and he flew straight to his father to tell him of the boys' cruelty.

The Wandjina called in a voice like thunder to all the earth's creatures to find the people so that they could be punished. Bicycle Lizard spotted the people and sped back to Wandjina who sent thunder, lightning and rain to the place. Most of the people drowned in the flood which followed. Two children rode to safety on a wallaby and joined those who had escaped. They cooked a fat kangaroo tail and made sweet leafsmoke in the fire, offering these things to Wandjina who stopped the rain. Wandjina left Dumbi and returned to his own country, Wanduli. There, at a place called Wanalirri, he is painted in the large rock shelter where he went into the earth. The children never touch owls now.

Some say the people who died were killed in a mighty battle with all the Wandjinas at Dumbai where they were outmanoeuvred and driven to their deaths on boggy ground. Others say that two of the boys who had tormented Dumbi hid in a hollow boab tree which, being a Wandjina,

Jagamurro, Ngarinyin *barnman* man.

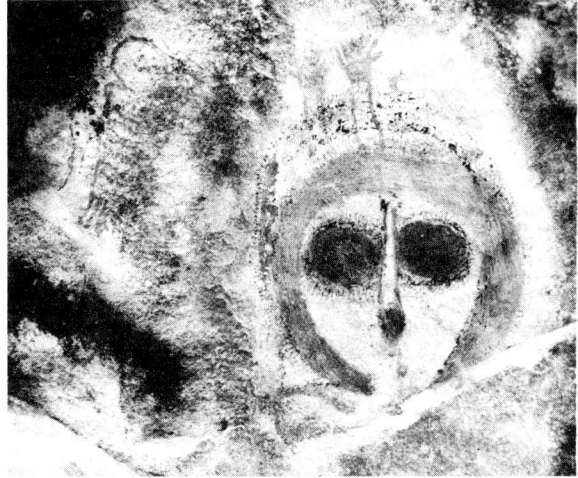

enclosed them and crushed them to death. It is all there, in ochre, on the Wanalirri rock.

Daisy Utemorrah sings with her people there, around the fire. One man has brought clapsticks and the rhythm must be piercing the night to the Gudurr place where the Wandjina struggled with the turtle. They sing many songs: about Dumbi, about a man who hunted a crocodile, about a turtle in the deep blue ocean. Some of these corroborees were composed long ago in the dreaming and some very recently — like the one about the dust from trucks. All people sing them.

The old man says, 'We dream about this. A spirit man comes and wakes you up. He says, ''Come, follow me, I'll show you a corroboree.'' Going up with the spirit man is good, but coming down is dangerous. You have to manage it properly. They give you everything to eat in the place where you make corroboree, but you say ''No'', because you want to come back home. If you touch spirit food you can't come back to earth again. In the changing place they teach you this'.

The Mowanjum people go on their way to Kalumburu just as the sun starts to warm the grass. We head towards Budbunjoningarri. Before we reach the *wumaral* firestick trees by the Gudurr place on the river we find the Wandjina's area, one of his rests on the way to Wanduli and the big shelter. Mowaljarlai says Wandjina had great shame, all that time ago, for killing the people. He walked to Wanduli, painting himself as he went to mark his way.

A wide *manduwal* path, cleared between rocks, leads to two outcrops with overhangs. On one we find Dumbi, hovering above the

The remains of someone returned to the Wandjina Banja at his place in Kimberley.

shoulder of the Wandjina who has two little arms with outstretched fingers reaching from the top of his head. Mowaljarlai says these are the hands of the boys who threw Dumbi in the air. There is another Wandjina image and two kangaroos with striped muzzles, whiskers and long eyelashes. Round the outcrop, a channel holds some long bones and skulls. These people have all gone back to Banja, the Wandjina of this place.

The other shelter yawns with the jaws of a crocodile. On the throat and the roof of the mouth all the Manangurr crocodiles twine their ochred bodies, their great Wandjina-eyes missing nothing. In the mouth a pile of stone eggs — 'Don't touch!' says Mowaljarlai. Above, towards the snout, an evil spirit looms. Mowaljarlai says the crocodile and the devil can paint together because they are both man killers, but the Wandjina will not paint on the same rock although he is close by. A long time ago, Manangurr crocodile ran with the fire, put it in the bush and burned the people. The *jalala* rock signs are all around this place for those who can see.

Far away, near the big river where the spirit children play on the white sand by the *wunggud* water, a great *mayangarri* stone stands tall in the ground. Its length joins Lejmarro, the milky way, with the earth. Jagamurro takes a pebble and remakes the eyes and the bullroarer line: after more than fifty years he has come back to Dilangarri to attend to the great sacred law stone. He sits and sings not far from a tree with spreading branches where sacred objects once

The *manduwal* path to the place of the Wandjina at Budbunjoningarri, Kimberley.

Manangurr crocodile images painted at Budbunjoningarri, Kimberley.

hung rattling in the breeze, their sound but not their sight allowed to women.

Jagamurro says that long, long ago, women made the law and kept the power of the sacred stone. Gorrai was jealous of their power and called Memej the great whirlwind to destroy them. Memej was a man but he was a whirlwind, too, and he came with awful force while Gorrai cursed the women who gave a great cry and turned themselves into stone in a circle around their sacred monument. Jagamurro sits now, singing this event, ringed by the smooth rock forms of the crouching Wongai women. Later, he says that ever since the women had

Rock enclosure overlooked by a Wandjina whose painted image has now almost disappeared: a temporary grave ringed by the name-stones of Ngarinyin tribesmen.

their power stolen they have been under the control of their husbands — 'Every man is Memej today'. And Memej stands now, a great white gum tree, guarding his work a short distance away, up the big river.

It is strangely still here. The spirit children play silently on the white sand by the *wunggud* water, waiting for their fathers to dream them and give them to their mothers. Mowaljarlai says, 'You dream them, you catch them in your hands; they say, ''I am waterlily, bat, stone, pandanus . . .'' They slip from your grasp and go into the womb and wait there. You know who they are, later, when they are born'.

To the southeast lies Wumbadengarri where a long rocky ridge curves through the bush. A faded Wandina is painted looking down from underneath a high shelter on to a grave-sized

The Wongai women turned themselves to stone at Dilangarri, Kimberley.

area marked with stones. A circle of many, many smaller stones stands outside, each carrying the name of a living Ngarinyin man. The scene is set. The dead man lies in the inner space, his feet towards the overhang, facing his Wandjina. The *barnman* doctor-man has peeled skin from the corpse and has seen on the pale surface the dark marks of disease or injury. He moves around the outer circle of stones, standing each one straight and calling its name. He addresses the dead man each time, 'Did this man kill you?' A few days later, the corpse has swelled and burst, sending out a stream of body fluid. The *barnman* man returns to examine the evidence — does any man's stone carry the stain of guilt? The Wandjina's gaze is impassive; such a man cannot escape his fate. It is the law.

35

The corpse is left in peace, protected from scavengers by a pile of rocks. Later, the mourners come and carry the body to the river where they wash the bones clean, paint them with ochre and put them in a coffin of paper bark bound with special string and annointed with fat. The white pipeclay paint is sprayed on from the mourners' mouths and all gather for the ceremony just before sunset. The two ritual poles stand apart, joined by the long hairstring. Dancers carry the special body designs in paint and fresh green leaves as they sing, 'Jirr, Jirr, Jirr — ahhh . . .', releasing the sorrow. Banggal, the bat, dances in and out on his painted wings. The hairstring is broken at sunset, releasing the dead man's spirit into the light and happiness of his family who will keep his bones with them for two cycles of the seasons. The Wandjina waits patiently to receive them in the rocks where he is painted. His faded image will be renewed by Jagamurro and Mowaljarlai before long. When they have received proper permission from the old men and women, they will bring the ochres back here.

Mowaljarlai says there is no ceremony for a woman. She goes back to the Wandjina and there is great sorrow for she is *mahmah*, like the Wandjina. She is the mother, the earth; she goes back to her own womb in the Wandjina where the spirits of men, servants of all that is *mahmah*, are received. Her knee prints, those of all women, are close by in the rocks, impressed by the thumb of the Wandjina when the earth was soft to remind all people of the joy, the pain and the responsibility of womankind.

Wanggangga, the sugar bag, is painted further along the ridge. The image carries the knowledge of that distant time when Wodoi and Jungun fought over the proper way to start the law for their people. Blood spilled in the fight made the ochre, and sugar bag honey, which Jungun mistakenly tried to use instead of emu fat to annoint the sacred object, is found everywhere in that place. Close by, the shadowy figures of the Janagun men move across the rock above the knee-marks of the world's mothers. They made the first spears, the same as those they gave to Jilingga when she was alive. She was painted in a special way in a cave on the coast where only married men could look at her. A red possum hides under a ledge below the Janagun men not far from a Wandjina whose feet have partly broken away with the rock on which they were painted.

Towards the west, in flat scrub country above the *wunggud* waters of the big river, Dalngna the king brown snake came up from the earth

Ngaleywan, Ngarinyin elder, at the Mandangarri place, Gibb River, Kimberley.

and left her image in stone. It marks the joining of the places of the snake people, the whirlwind people and the black-eyed cuckoo people. She went on, marking the territory and urinating, leaving signs and *wunggud* pools. As she went on to new places, she taught the people their different languages and songs and gave them the law. When Dalngna came to the crow people, she found them using a fire-burned woomera to circumcise their initiates. She said, 'This is wrong, you hurt the child', and blew her nose on the ground where the mucus turned to stone. The people have used a sharp stone for this part of initiation ever since.

At Nyalanggunda, the great *wunggud* place of the Mandangarri snakes, the ochre images writhe in interlocking patterns in the mouth of a rock overhang. Ngaleywan points to the painted women among the images — they are the keepers of the snake dreaming. Across a grassy space, boulders of the saliva of the snake crown a similar outcrop. But the sun is sinking and we hurry back through the rocky scrub — the Wandjina waits at Wanalirri in his final resting place some hours away where we will see him tomorrow. Wanalirri gorge is deep and dangerous; we are exhausted by the climb down. Ngaleywan has already called to the Wandjina from the top, announcing the visit and asking him not to be angry about it. As we drop down from boulder to boulder, the images on the long shelter walls become clearer and Ngaleywan frowns at some dark clouds forming on the horizon at the gorge's end. We sit at last on the earth floor, face to face with the long image of Wojin, and he looks through us to the gorge bottom where we felt him so strongly.

There are so many images of the Wandjina here, in rows like soldiers returned from the battle at Dumbai. Wojin floats above them showing, over his shoulder, a branch of his berry tree. Galaru snake images lie on the warm rock among the sugar bags, kangaroos and other creatures. Two grey and red figures look like women giving birth; Ngaleywan says they are lightning spirits. A Ngonol image, spirit of the wind and cyclone, stands with upraised arms near two Juwa evil spirits who crush the heads of children with rocks. After that, says Mowaljarlai, the children go mad and become wanderers; plenty of them die, not just young children, older ones too. The Wandjina representing Mowaljarlai is there with two black cockatoo feathers standing up from his head; he is Yaobada, the thunderer. Barberi stands next to him and Deluk, wife of Ngaleywan, flanks two other female Wandjinas who can hold back or divert the rain and gather up the clouds to bring rain to flood out people who do not share properly. The dark clouds seem to recede as we toil out of the gorge; there is no sign of them when we eventually reach the track.

Lejmarro reflects on earth, in Ngarinyin coun-

Great sandstone boulders balance for ages along the way.

try, the milky way: for every law, two witnesses. This is the way it is, and you go on your feet, north of the Caroline Ranges: an old way and a long way. There is a place there that reflects a great star of Ngarinyin law. Jagamurro cannot come and we follow Mowaljarlai down from the range, leaving behind the little truck in a firebreak we have cleared. The grass reaches our shoulders and, in less than two hours, Mowaljarlai has led us over gullies and hills to Dinggal-Darr-Mumangarri, where the two long bones stand in stone image. These are the *wung-gud* bones of Yahmarro, the great red kangaroo, who marked this place in his travels. We follow his path, past the smooth rock incline made by the *wunggud* female kangaroo as she passed and left her image there, ground in the polished rock floor. The huge sandstone boulders mount in crazy piles all around; the *jalala* rock signs draw us on to the place where Yahmarro is painted on the shoulders of the Wandjina Wahmaj Muli Muli. They are the same: *wunggud*, and the power made everything.

Yahmarro — Walamba — ran from the hunters all that time ago. He ran all across the top of Australia, down the coast and here to Dinggal. The hunters chased him down to the bottom of the country. He was lonely, he looked back. The stamp-stamp-stamp of the hunters' feet had ceased; he heard no chant of 'Yah. Yah. Yah!' — 'Come back, we need to catch you'. Yahmarro swung around to Uluru — Ayers Rock — where he left his final skull and foot marks. His image place here at Dinggal was painted by Wahmaj Muli Muli whose son stands at Yahmarro's head with the footprints of all the *yahmarro*. Behind Yahmarro his wives stand in a group while four more of Wahmaj Muli Muli's sons watch from another outcrop of rock. Old Wumbagun is *gugai* — custodian — of this place and its knowledge. He shares the responsibility with some other, very old, Ngarinyin men. We sleep round a fire in the soft sand near a drying waterhole where *yahmarro* stretch down to drink.

At dawn we start a long walk, Mowaljarlai reading the *jalala* signals to the sugar bag painting place. A long, straight natural pathway flanked by those huge, wildly balanced sandstone boulders takes us northeast for an hour. Several of them hide small paintings in their caves: a little sugar bag, fish spirits and the slim Winjin cyclone spirits. The sugar bag image is painted large on the back wall of the overhang. Beneath it, tucked into the space between the wall and the earth floor, layered paper bark coffins erode into dust. Some bones have spilled on

The Wandjina lies above a shelter in Lejmarro, Kimberley.

to the floor: the femur of a large man lies in a scatter of ochred finger bones not far from what seem to be the skull and ribs of a small child. Many people have returned to the Wandjina who lies above the shelter entrance and *wonggi* initiates have changed here, too. But people lived and worked here as well. To either side of the curving shelter, the flakes of stone have fallen as men sat on the rocks making the tiny black barbs for the Jungun spears and the fine pink Wodoi points. Many, many generations of women have used the large grinding slabs to feed their families. The debris from thousands of fires and meals, from the tool making, the burials and the ceremonies has helped to raise the level of the floor, and the two red and black snake images seem to rise from the dirt against the back wall. Pieces of ochre, some with facets rubbed on them, lie with the other discarded things of the living and dying of so many people.

Mowaljarlai learns still, and must learn fast, for those old *gugai* are preparing to die, some very soon. Many have taken untaught knowledge with them to their Wandjinas at the end of lives dislocated by forced removal from their homes. No one man can carry the whole learning of a people, but there are other Ngarinyin people, younger than Mowaljarlai, who have already learned much and will learn more.

# 4
# ABOUT MAKING AND KEEPING ROCK PAINTINGS

Painted figures hide in a shelter in Cape York.

There is one small rock shelter with a scatter of fading stencils — hands, weapons, small creatures — a few painted human figures and some engraved animal tracks. It was a place of great significance to generations of people. No living person knows anything about that place now except by analogy with other places and their people. Another shelter, in another place, also lies quietly watching the seasons pass. This is very large, its wide stage swarming with colourful characters whose intricate decorations, dancing movements, strange forms and charming and bizarre features attract a constant trickle of determined visitors. This place, too, was once of great significance to a group of people now scattered or dead. The difference between the two places lies not in their importance to the people who made and kept them and their art, but simply in their appeal to the eyes of other people. The art of the second place is better for outsiders to look at.

By and large, the photographs in this book have been chosen because they are beautiful, not because they are stylistically or geographically representative, although they serve this purpose to an extent. Some have an importance which is really not known at all and some illustrate stories which are still told and support ritual which is still enacted.

The people of some Australian societies did not paint or engrave rock surfaces at all, even though suitable rock may have been available. Groups north and west of the Darling River in New South Wales engraved rock and made special stone arrangements. To the south, people painted on rock walls and ceilings while groups further east carved their designs on the trunks of trees. Some groups in other places apparently chose not to express themselves on rock — it was not, and did not become, part of their way.

An 'art site' is any place where an instance of art occurs. It may be the place where a carved tree grows, a boulder with pecked-out bird tracks on it, or a shelter with ochre paintings. Paintings and engravings can occur at the same site, of course, and a shelter may contain one painted figure or hundreds. Lesley Maynard counted about 100 000 engravings in one square kilometre in the Pilbara, and nearly 300 000 figures in the various techniques have been counted in New South Wales alone. This may be as many as half of the pictures which are actually there in that State.

The pictures in this book were painted or drawn using colours from a variety of sources. Ochre seems to be the pigment used most often.

Red ochre is very widely used and comes in a variety of shades from pink through brilliant hues to red-browns and purples. There are many stories that tell how deposits of ochre resulted from the spilled blood of spirit ancestors. Thuwathu, the rainbow serpent, bled not far from Jalga-Gindidbu on Mornington Island, and Wodoi and Jungun, when they fought in Ngarinyin country left the blood from their wounds as ochre in a range above the big river. There are many, many places, but not every group has such a place in their country: many peoples had to barter and travel for their ochre and for other pigments. Everywhere, people's campfires supplied as much charcoal as they needed for their art, but apparently manganese oxide was also used, and traded, to get black colour. White is often obtained from pipeclay, which is widely available, but gypsum and burnt selenite are used, too.

As well as the range of reds, minerals can be found which produce blue and yellow. Professor Elkin records glauconite as the source of blue paint in Kimberley. Yellow has a number of sources including yellow limonite, burnt red limonite oxide, dust from ants' nests and a particular fungus. Some single silhouetted figures near Laura in Cape York are painted in a brilliant orange which, according to P.J. Trezise, is one of the naturally occurring ochre colours in that area. Red is the colour which seems to be of the greatest importance. F.D. McCarthy deals in his handbook with the technology of both rock engraving and painting. He describes the ochre mine at Wilga Mia in Western Australia, most remarkable of the Australian ochre mines, with its open cut excavations, tunnels following the seams of red and yellow pigment, and pole scaffolds. It had most likely been worked over thousands of years and was still in use in 1939. Besides natural ochre veins, various shades of red were obtained from laterites, limonites, manganese, iron oxide, ferruginous sandstone and certain creekbed gravels. Yellow ochre, prophyry and trap rocks can be burnt to make red colours and they can be collected as powder from rock surfaces or from the inside of silica nodules. The small sacs in the bulbous root of a sundew plant also provided red pigment in parts of South Australia.

Sometimes, pigments such as charcoal, ochre or clay may be applied, dry, to the rock surface, as with a crayon. A small piece of pigment could also be wetted and fixed on the end of a length of stout grass stem or a pointed wooden 'skewer' to give control in applying fine points or lines to decoration. Green twigs, their ends chewed to produce a brush, make a range of line thicknesses possible and these, together with brushes made by binding feathers or hairs on a stem, were perhaps the most used painting tools in Australia. Paint is made by mixing powdered pigment with water, fat, or, as in Arnhem Land, orchid juice which acts as a fixative. Ochres and other hard pigments may be crushed between mortar stones or rubbed directly on a mortar to produce powder. The artist's finger may be used to apply thick lines or fill small areas with colour. The whole hand can be used to apply background 'washes', as in the white backgrounds to Wandjina and snake paintings in Kimberley (Plate 6). Stencils, of hands, weapons or other objects, are made by blowing mixed paint from the mouth. Paint splatters, or spots, are also blown from the mouth over painted figures, and the paper bark coffin pouches of Kimberley are decorated this way.

The rock itself is part of the whole 'ways and means' of rock art — a medium, just like a canvas or a piece of bark. A rock painting figure, painted in ochre on a piece of paper or a plank of wood would not look the same at all. The effect of ochre on rock has not yet been mentioned; the effect of rock on ochre is perhaps more to the point. Sandstone is probably the rock that has been used most often for painting. Great escarpments with huge overhangs weathered in their sides are classical art sites, but smaller outcrops — even quite tiny, isolated ones — may be even more important if people have little rock to work on. Quartzite formations are used, as well as granite, limestone, slate and other kinds of rock.

Rock and ochre come together in ways often visually breathtaking. Sandstone, especially, soaks up colour, and a figure or group may have as a background what seem to be the coloured spirits of forms long taken into the rock and now somehow indistinguishable from it. The remains of disappearing figures seem to provide features in strange landscapes where newer forms stand or dance. This can be seen in Plate 36. Snake-like figures wriggle into or out of natural holes and crevices, and surface dents or bumps form features of beings. Figures curve into or are framed by areas of newer surface left as pieces of the old slide off.

These things can be seen well enough on a photograph; but sometimes figures loom over a shelter, bending from wall to ceiling in a way that can only really be appreciated by — and was only intended for — those standing or lying in the shelter. The camera usually flattens the image. Figures float over the craggy contours of the rock in wraithlike perspective which, too, is sometimes lost on the camera. The rock is not the medium or the 'frame' in any sense that can be isolated, it is as much a part of the art as are the figures and it was never intended to be seen through a camera — no art is. But the camera is still the best of the alternative methods of 'seeing' art, although rock art must be among the most difficult forms to photograph. At times it is downright dangerous. Sometimes it seems that only a spirit could have painted in places so high and inaccessible to ordinary mortals. Sensible conclusions about artists painting from the branches of trees long since dead and untraceable do not really dispel this illusion.

Conserving Australian rock art — keeping it for the future — has been much discussed and written about in the last decade: the present state of paintings and other kinds of pictures, the destructive forces operating on them and the possibilities, plans and agencies for their preservation. The past, present and future destruction of rock art sites and their paintings is of two kinds: natural and political. Natural forces have taken an accelerating toll of rock art as a direct result of the operation of political forces over the past two hundred years. This has everywhere destroyed the cultural integrity of Aboriginal societies and has achieved two things. It has acquired a vast body of cultural material and turned it into the inheritance of a new nation by dispossessing its natural inheritors of the rights and responsibilities of its management, and it has made the artificial conservation of cultural material an imperative as a direct result.

In recent years a great deal of information about the physical facts of rock painting has been collected by many people, mostly academics, from disciplines such as archaeology, geology and museology. Shelters have been examined and information recorded about drainage patterns, rock types and stability, tree and plant root incursion, moulds, lichen, the effects of direct and indirect rock weathering, and of human and insect activity. Rates of weathering are difficult to determine: they vary at individual sites and even at different spots on one shelter wall. It is possible to say that a given painting is likely to last longer than another and it is also possible to reduce weathering at particular sites by reducing their exposure to weathering agents such as water. This can be done by draining. But weathering cannot be halted: sooner or later all rock paintings will disappear. Protective measures of the various kinds which have been devised and implemented as a result of the study of painted rock surfaces can only delay the inevitable.

Destructive forces of the natural kind include water, wind, sun, dust and fire, as well as insect, bird and animal activity. The activities of tourists may cause accidental damage, as with dust from vehicle wheels or smoke from picnic fires, or deliberate damage resulting from unthinking actions or plain vandalism. J. Clarke notes, for Kimberley, at least, the sad fact that human vandalism is probably the main cause of rock art deterioration. Water erosion is often nominated as the predominant cause of damage to rock paintings. Edwards believes it accounts for about seventy per cent of all damage. In the northern areas of Australia, where humidity is high and the annual monsoonal rainfall can be greater than 1400 millimetres, a great deal of this kind of damage occurs.

Painting on exposed rock washes and weathers away very quickly and this is probably one of the reasons why almost all the rock paintings recorded are in shelters of various kinds — mostly rock overhangs. The effects of water on these are not consistent. They vary from season to season and, as erosion takes place, new patterns of drainage and seepage form. New damp conditions encourage plants to send out their roots to new places and provide moulds and lichen with pleasant homes. Sometimes these happen to be built on top of ochre paintings. The roots of plants not only cling to rock walls and cover and destroy any paintings in their way, but also prise open crevises to make new paths for water seepage. Shelters that have excellent drip-lines and are protected from the direct effects of rainfall often fall victim to seepage.

On rocks that are not very porous, such as hard quartzites, paintings are washed away easily. But where ochres have been given time to sink into the structure of the rock, water damage, at least, is not such a threat. However, this does not stop mould and lichen from growing over them if they are in damp places. As it happens, the people themselves preferred large, airy shelters where damp was not a problem. Still, in cases where these were not available, people had to make do with less-than-ideal shelters. Lichen is particularly destructive because its growth generates humic acid which attacks the quartz grains of the rock and can stain them green, permanently. When drainage patterns change, previously dry shelters can become damp and provide not only new homes for moulds and lichen but also provide, in the form of mud, the material for the nests of insects. There are paintings which have been almost completely covered by the home-making activities of termites and other insects. Termites are more active in damp shelters than dry ones; ants build nests on the ground close to the base of shelter walls and gradually exend them up the rock face. The larger, individual mud nests of wasps can be found dotted in their dozens over painted figures.

Heat from the sun causes flaking of pigments, especially where they have not been absorbed into the rock. The white clay background wash of many Kimberley paintings does not penetrate the rock the way well-prepared ochres do and, when they flake or wash away, they take the painted figures with them. The sun dries grass and undergrowth which accumulates in and around unlived-in shelters and, if this catches fire, paintings are burned and blackened by soot. Wind-blown dust and sand also cause damage.

The number of animals who might enjoy a good scratch on rocks which may have paintings on them has increased in the last two hundred years. Where previously kangaroos and wallabies might deposit dirt and rub away ochre as they scratched or brushed against shelter walls, now buffalo, goats, pigs and horses have swelled the number of participants in this pleasurable activity.

The Reverend John Mathew was speaking about a Victorian painting site in 1896. He notes that, 'The outlines are weather-worn and in various places it is next to impossible to distinguish them from the red blotches naturally in the stone'. He refers to Messrs Muirhead and Carter, who 'discovered' the paintings in 1866. The latter, he says, ' . . . affirms that they look [then, in 1896] just about as fresh as when first seen. This is not surprising, as they are perfectly protected from rain'. The Reverend Mathew introduces a new problem, however, when he observes that, 'The difficulty of copying has been increased through the ambition of white people to secure a cheap fame by scribbling over the Aboriginal work with charcoal. One feels indignant that so rare a relic of Aboriginal art should be wantonly desecrated and defaced.'

Over the years a lot more paintings have been defaced in a number of ways by individuals overly concerned with their egos or their souvenir collections. Improved communications have extended the venues of these activities until even the most remote places are at risk from them. Besides these personalised contributions to their destruction, paintings have increasingly got in the way of material progress. Road, railway and pipeline construction has wiped sites away, developers and town planners have done the same and advertisers have put up billboards and signs at rock art sights to cash in on the fact that people visit these places to look at the paintings.

Meanwhile, compromise measures, both physical and legislative, have been effected. Painted shelters have been fitted with protective barriers to minimise direct damage by people in heavily visited areas. Cars and cooking fires are kept at a distance to reduce dust, smoke and other pollution levels. Shelters have sometimes been artificially drained so that water damage is less of a hazard. It has not been possible, so far, to apply widely any kind of substance which would strengthen and protect painted surfaces effectively. The problems here are mostly to do with unknown long-term effects of such treatment, although analysis of the factors involved is progressing.

In Kimberley, a number of test sites are being monitored by J. Clarke after being treated with a low concentration of silicone resin. This was done after a number of tests on artificially-produced samples. The problem to be overcome was the damaging effect of the capilliary action of water passing in or out of the pigment layer. A thin layer of the silicone resin coats the pigment particles and prevents capilliary action, but allows vapour to pass freely. This treatment stabilises the rock surface. Lichen growth, too, has been successfully removed and its regrowth deterred by the careful use of a broad-spectrum, amine-based herbicide. The Australian National Parks and Wildlife Service is also doing this kind of monitoring work in Kakadu National Park, Northern Territory, where P. J. Hughes recently investigated the causes and effects of mechanical deterioration of rock art in the area and provided recommendations for programmes of protection and management of sites. These sorts of reports have been commissioned in a number of places in Australia.

Aboriginal material culture, and particularly rock art, is seen by most authorities as a valuable resource. Its value is generally understood to be bound up with that of tourism and with that accruing from a better scientific knowledge of the world. But tourists and tourism are gradually destroying the things that bring them, and the revenue they create, to particular places, and the scientists face a dilemma in the advice they offer the State on matters of preservation. To be effective, conservation measures would often logically entail that both tourism and development cease in particular areas and that sites be given back into the care of the people whose right they are. There is, however, no halting the great cultural devastation which has already occurred through the destruction of Aboriginal societies. In some places there is no question of being able to hand back their material culture to people who still function in terms of it. But even where possible this has hardly ever been done. Among Aboriginal people, even in the southern States where they have been longest dislocated culturally and have had greatest involvement in European systems of education and politics, there are very many who understand their own peoples' ways and values well. A great number of known sites are of direct cultural significance to Aboriginals, and others are significant by birthright. Outside decisions are an offence against these rights, and at last an Aboriginal view is beginning to be expressed which challenges the entire ethical basis of 'foreign' political control over the conservation, protection and exploitation of rock art. There are also many other people — scientists, politicians and private individuals — who see the ideological problem fairly clearly, but the weight of official opinion is heavy.

In 1973, at a national seminar convened by the Institute for the Conservation of Cultural Material, there were a number of papers given which focussed on rock art. C. Pearson of the Western Australian Museum defined the problem as deterioration of rock art and went on to recommend detailed examination of the causes (weathering, vandals, atmospheric pollutants, insects etc) through scientific research in geology, geomorphology, mineralogy, climatology and laboratory analysis of samples of painted rock surfaces. Given adequate staff, facilities and expertise, the results of such examinations should lead to better measures for the conservation of rock art in the field. This analysis of the problem and recommendation for action was prefaced with the statement that, 'Very few Aboriginal paintings are today being painted or even touched up and if rapid and effective action is not taken within the next decade then a vast number of paintings will be lost'. Perhaps the problem, in many cases, is being defined in quite the wrong terms. The Western Australian Museum has legal responsibility for the protection and preservation of Aboriginal sites in Western Australia and these include, most significantly, the painted sites in Kimberley. There the old owners of sites can and do visit some painting places and restore paintings and stone arrangements, travelling long distances largely on their own initiative and with quite inadequate resources except of determination.

S. Walston, after presenting to the 1973 seminar a plan, since implemented, for the

A protective cage erected at a shelter at Mt Grenfell, New South Wales.

protection by drainage of paintings at Mt Grenfell, New South Wales, makes the point that although conservation techniques can reduce the rate of deterioration of rock art, they cannot stop it. She goes on: 'Perhaps the only final and responsible method for ensuring the survival of Aboriginal art is to encourage those qualified in the skills derived from Aboriginal culture to repaint or restore the paintings'. More guarded is P. J. Hughes's opinion that, quickly and effectively implemented, protection measures, '. . . would perhaps allow sufficient time for some of the moral and technical problems associated with the preservation of rock art to be resolved'.

Lesley Maynard sets out to tackle the problem head-on, pointing out the differences in values attached to art by Aboriginals and Europeans. European values of personal creative expression and permanence of art objects do not apply to Aboriginal works, and so ideas of desecration are quite different. She points out that to restore a damaged Leonardo da Vinci by retouching it with fresh paint, no matter how skilfully, would be considered desecration; a disturbance of the

integrity of the artist's creation. This notion is alien to Aboriginal art which is remade or restored as the occasion demands. Specific paintings, such as Wandjina images in Kimberley and figures in Central Australia are restored at each turn of the ceremonial cycle. There are older figures under many Wandjina paintings. In other areas such as Cape York and in New South Wales, new paintings were made regularly, often covering parts of older figures. None of this is desecration to Aboriginals who have a quite different view of the purpose of this work from that of Europeans who have labelled it 'art', attached alien values to it and who have consequently been known to wring their hands when confronted by a beautifully decorated figure surmounted and partly obliterated by a roughly-executed one.

Conservation of rock paintings is undertaken now as though they are the same sort of cultural idea as a Leonardo da Vinci when, in fact, they were made to be replaced or restored by those with the clearly-defined right. Maynard therefore suggested that *restoration* be considered as a possible method for maintaining rock paintings or treating damaged ones. She noted that there were still Aboriginals who knew how to paint on rocks and bark, also that Europeans know a lot about the role of art in Aboriginal societies and about its techniques. While she stopped short of saying *who* should mix, match and carefully apply the correct pigments in any given instance of restoration, the implication that Aboriginal people could apply their inherited cultural expertise in many instances was clear.

In a paper entitled 'The Involvement of the Aboriginal People in the Conservation of their Sites and Culture', Howard Creamer of the National Parks and Wildlife Service, New South Wales, drove home his contention that 'involving the Aboriginal people in all ventures that concern them is now the essential ingredient of success itself'. He understood well that his assertion was an unpopular one, even with some conservationists in 1973. Those at the seminar who viewed such developments as 'an unwelcome chimera to be thwarted on the battleground of bureaucracy and technical bafflement' he advised to think again. He set out a scheme for Aboriginal involvement in decision-making, planning and active participation in conservation of their sites of all kinds. This was backed up in a paper by Ray Kelly, a Thangetti man employed as a Research Officer with National Parks and Wildlife Service, New South Wales, who said, 'I believe there is only one way left for we Aboriginals to restore our culture, and that is

44

by getting all the old men together and letting them guide us on which is the best way to preserve our culture'. Creamer's scheme had been in operation for a few months at that time and has continued and gained strength in New South Wales over subsequent years where its main focus, at the direction of the Aboriginal people, has been the attempt to protect recent burial grounds and important ceremonial grounds from the demands of modern development.

An International Workshop on the Conservation of Rock Art was organised in Perth in 1977 by the Institute for the Conservation of Cultural Material. The thirty-three delegates, including four Aboriginals and five people from overseas countries with rock art, heard seventeen papers dealing with the scientific recording and conservation of rock art.

Apart from a short introductory paper by W. Dix of the Australian Institute of Aboriginal Studies, only one paper discussed traditional owners. In relation to a well-known, quickly deteriorating Northern Territory rock art site, G. Chaloupka says, 'This site should be visited in the company of the traditional owners, some of whom are said to be rock painters, and paintings and engravings, with their help, recorded and described and the necessary conservation measures discussed with them'. Dix points out that, 'It is as indefensible to assume control over Aboriginal art sites — on whatever pretext — as it was to assume control over land 200 years ago . . . at least where the sites retain traditional significance the Aboriginal control should be total'. This is not to advocate abdication of responsibility by government authorities: that responsibility is clear and the resources in its service, although inadequate, must be used to conserve rock art by the best means available. It is only in a proportion of cases now that actual restoration work could be left in the expert hands of Aboriginal artists.

Within the last decade all Australian States except the Australian Capital Territory have enacted legislation which provides for the conservation of Aboriginal relics through specific authorities. These carry on cultural resource management programmes and employ archaeologists and other administrators. Investigation and recording of sites, employment and training of rangers, surveys of visitor-use and behaviour, provision of advice on conservation measures and the implementation of these are among the usual responsibilities of these bodies. Aboriginal people have generally been encouraged to undertake training as rangers and site recorders.

P. F. J. Coutts, reviewing in 1978 a decade of cultural resource management in Australia, says, 'In all instances, the various pieces of legislation which are current have been shown to be inadequate. Many of these shortcomings have evolved through the emasculation of the Acts as a result of political pressures. The administrative arrangements which support the Acts are their worst aspects — they are generally weak and inappropriate'. Even in the States where Aboriginal involvement is most encouraged, its effectiveness is limited by the weakness of the administrative structures and their lack of adequate resources. Always, at whatever level, it is only involvement. It can never become control since it is tied into administrative structures whose titular managers are themselves not given a real brief to control the protection and conservation of Aboriginal cultural material. The rights of Aboriginal people to climb even this shaky ladder was apparently in doubt as late as 1978. Coutts remarked then that, 'Like any other group of Australians, Aborigines have the right to demand that their cultural legacy is protected and, while whites may remain apathetic about helping to protect this legacy, Aborigines have a good case for being included in the organisations which administer that legacy'.

The gathering Coutts was addressing in 1978, a UNESCO Regional Seminar on Preserving Indigenous Cultures (published 1980) agreed that:

The Seminar recognised the right of the Australian Aborigines and Torres Strait Islanders to continue their own way of life and retain their own cultural traditions. The meeting recognised also that the ultimate authority for the traditions of the different groups belonged to the leaders at the local community level.

Participants believed that in considering the culture of the Australian Aboriginal and Islander people, the greatest sacred thing was the land itself and in particular the sacred sites within the land and its surrounding areas; the right of the elders and recognised leaders to own and control these sites must be recognised by all persons.

However, these acknowledgements and beliefs were not among the matters communicated officially by the Seminar to the Australian Federal Government. The list of resolutions sent urged more support for museums in their pursuit of the preservation of indigenous cultures. Resolutions directed to the Australian national commission for UNESCO mostly urged consideration of Aboriginal involvement in museum activities and projects.

Recording, analysis, trialling and monitoring has continued through the various State bodies and advice on conservation has been given to governments. Art sites are only a portion of the total of sites of significance to the Aboriginal people. Where the sites are also significant to governments in terms of tourism or the somewhat confused notion of 'national heritage' alone, advice is often accepted and implemented. Where advice conflicts with plans for other kinds of land use, such as building, communications or mining, the 'national heritage' may be seen to consist in a different set of acquisitions. Coutts notes that, 'Politics continues to play a significant role . . . Sites are simply not looked for or declared, because the authorities fear delays could occur to development projects and they are apprehensive of the costs involved in the protection and perhaps investigation of archaeological sites'.

As well as the State bodies officially responsible for the administration of legislation on conservation of Aboriginal material culture, and the work done to this end in museums and universities, special bodies exist to deal with particular aspects of Aboriginal cultures. The Australian Institute of Aboriginal Studies records and keeps much material, and the Aboriginal Arts Board of the Australia Council works to keep the flame of traditional practice burning. The Board's members are all Aboriginal and its aim is to support all Aboriginal cultural expression and identity — old and new — through the arts. It has also given considerable support to seminars and training schemes in the conservation of material culture set up by other institutions. There are plans for a rock art museum at a major engraving site in the Sydney area where the art is not part of a living culture. Museums have been set up in Europe at Late Paleolithic cave art sites where the art, as in Sydney, is prehistoric. Where art is part of a living culture, plans for such museums can have unconscionable moral consequences for the Aboriginal people as well as reflecting badly on the legitimate concerns of museums. The story of 'Billy's Cave', told in *Killing Me Softly* by P. and N. Wallace illustrates this.

Even in European terms, insufficient attention is being paid to the conservation of rock art in Australia, as a recent editorial in the ICCM Bulletin points out:

> It is one of the ironies of conservation priorities that while the multimillion dollar Art Gallery of Australia nears completion in Canberra, many Aboriginal rock art sites are nearing obliteration in multimillion dollar developments on the other side of Australia. In this case the threatened sites are in the Dampier archipelago of Western Australia where natural gas processing facilities claim a better right to the land than rock carvings which have been there for thousands of years.

But even rock carvings still apparently claim a better right to the land than their makers and the descendants of their makers. These people have, in many places in Australia, breathed real cultural life into what would otherwise have joined the host of dead Aboriginal objects and archaeological relics. In fact, many of these things and places are nevertheless defined as relics in the various Acts. The people have been used to put the stories with the pictures in museum displays, exhibitions and books. In many places they and their knowledge could also be used to restore rock paintings according to an enlightened approach to conservation in a society which may never know better than to use all people and all things in the pursuit of more things.

The Federal Government is being urged to set up an emergency fund to bring back into the country Aboriginal cultural material which has been given or sold overseas. The aims are to consolidate and display the enormous Aboriginal contribution to Australia's cultural heritage: the unique sights, sounds and ideas of ancient cultures salvaged for posterity by their new owners while those who 'contributed' them struggle for basic human rights in their own country.

# 5
# SOME PLACES,
# STYLES
# AND STORIES

Kimberley landscape.

## Kimberley

Countless wets and countless dries have come and gone over the mountains, rivers and little plains of Kimberley. They are watched over and directed by the Wandjina spirits who live in all the land, waiting forever in the gorges, by the mountains, in the *wunggud* waters of rivers and pools; on the rock where they painted themselves long ago. Wandjinas, in their human form with a halo of cloud and lightning, great eyes and mysterious emptiness where a mouth might be, rest in rock shelters along the far northwestern coast, on islands and among the mountains to the east where the big rivers run.

They are not alone in their long vigil; Wandjinas of the inland and the Kaiara who came across the sea from the northwest, have company of many kinds. Spirits rest in ochre as snakes, crocodiles, fish, kangaroos and other creatures. Their symbols take the form of tracks, excreta, rocks of saliva and eggs. Other spirits of different kinds join in the paintings. Some are always evil; they are grotesque and pounce or caper on the rock at a distance from the calm centre guarded by the Wandjina. Sometimes spirits of the cyclone or storm rest by themselves in their shelters (Plate 12) as do sugar bags (wild honey). Sometimes people — men and women — seem to be there. The *wunggud* spirit is there in all sorts of images.

There are a lot of people who know a lot about *wunggud* matters in Kimberley. Some of them have told some of it to outsiders. The painted images are a focus of all this knowledge. I. M. Crawford knows as much as any living outsider about such things. He feels that the great Wandjinas in human form — some are about seven metres long — are beings in the clouds. Clouds are Wandjina images: the part of nature most under Wandjina control, but the people know that, at one time, Wandjinas travelled on the earth like people until, unlike people, they entered the earth at places where their images are left on rock. The people relate that the Wandjinas created their own paintings on the rocks. Since the humans inherited the images from the spirits it has been their duty to repair damage caused by water, wind and the activities of insects and other creatures, and respect the places and images of Wandjina.

Wandjinas (in the plural because it is not clear to what extent or on what level they are one spirit) are the central characters in the painted records of their lives and deeds. A complex body of knowledge tells of their travels. Their paths cross and recross over Kimberley linking many groups of people who hold the many parts of the great epic. So complicated is this pattern that it would be impossible to untangle but for the mighty battle at Dumbai in which the Wandjinas fought and vanquished the people so long ago. This battle is told of by nearly all people and was mentioned in Chapter 3. It acts as a point of reference in the stories of Wandjina travels: some events took place before the Wandjinas were summoned by Wojin to the battle, some afterwards as they resumed their travels and finally came to the places where their bodies went into the earth (Plates 7, 8).

The spirits of the Wandjina are immortal, like the spirits of ordinary people. But they are powerful and must be treated with great respect for they can avenge disrespect in terrible ways, through flood and storm. They have charge of some of the spirits of children who wait for their parents in the *wunggud* waters of rivers and pools. The spirits with snake images, keep children's spirits for certain people, as do crocodiles for others. People come from Wandjina and ask the Wandjina, through song, for the rains that fill the rivers and provide food for all creatures.

The knowledge tells of a time before the Wandjinas came, a time when different customs prevailed, but we know little about it. Rituals associated with the Wandjina are spoken of but, apart from rain-songs, the words are all we have. Perhaps, now that certain people are able to return to their Wandjinas to restore their paintings, the ceremonies will once again be arranged to mark those occasions.

All the Wandjinas have at least one name. Men and women carry the name of the Wandjina from whom their baby spirit came. In Ngarinyin country in the centre of Kimberley lies the gorge and shelter of Wanalirri where Wojin carries the plum tree branch and his followers are painted along his body (Plates 7, 8). There are two groups of Wandjina images, those at the western end all being described as Galaru. Although all the Wandjinas who fought the people at Dumbai are painted at Wanalirri, most of them went on to the west leaving Wojin himself there. Their paths crossed on the way to the coast where the Kaiara had remained. These Kaiara sea Wandjinas were among the few groups who did not travel to central Kimberley to fight in the battle at Dumbai. Their images are painted in coastal places.

At two of the coastal sites Crawford has found evidence for style changes. These are hard to find at Wandjina sites, because paintings have a white background applied first which tends to hide things underneath. The most recent figure at one site has a background which barely extends beyond the Wandjina and is incomplete at the head end. The earlier Wandjinas are in a slightly different style as is also the case at another site where small Wandjinas and fishes are painted over an older, larger Wandjina.

In 1837 George Grey was looking for an inland sea in Kimberley when he came upon a Wandjina painting. He was taken aback to find himself observed by the gigantic figure which seemed to stand out from the rock and loom over him. He saw and sketched a group of four Wandjina women and another single male figure which he described, in 1837, as ancient. His sketch of this figure caused quite a swell of speculation because it showed the figure clothed in a single garment reaching from neck to ankle and wrists, and what looked like ancient script on the halo. A century later, when other workers visited the area and took photographs of Wandjina images, it was easy to see how the ceremonial decorations on all full Wandjina figures could have been interpreted by Grey as clothing. But, in the meantime, the imaginations of scholars had run riot over a gamut of possible 'intruders' represented by the Wandjina, from Macassans, Malays and Sumatrans through Moors and Japanese to Hindus. The 'script' on the 'turban' was even interpreted — in two ancient languages. Still, when Crawford photographed Grey's figure well over a century later, it seemed, badly deteriorated though it was, to be perfectly at home in the Wandjina style. The markings on the halo seem to have been caused by the cracking and peeling of successive layers of paint.

The snake images and the Wandjinas are closely associated, often in a way that makes it difficult to know where the *idea* of one ends and the other begins. The snakes are often painted on a white background in the same basic style as Wandjinas, being heavy, somehow — not lithe and graceful even when they are shown coiled. In this style, it is not at all surprising to find a Wandjina human image amongst them, as at the Mandangarri place (Plate 6). There are snakes sharing the shelter at Wanalirri, some like those at Mandangarri and some not. There, at Wanalirri, the Wandjinas at the western end of the shelter were described as Galaru, a word used for snake. These large snakes, often referred to as pythons, do not seem to be named in nature as, for instance, the stories of other travels name the king brown snake. Perhaps, like the Wandjinas, they are no longer abroad on the earth. Again like Wandjina, they are associated with

the weather, spirit children and fertility, but they are especially associated with water — *wunggud* water. This is good when spirit children are given, but can be very dangerous for people going into or crossing such water.

Many snakes came from Mondol in the south towards the Gibb River. In an open space by a spring, they decided that Gunjud should stay to look after that place. Manuwala went with her little daughter to Wunggarun, a place not far away, on a creek, where she lay on her back in the water and made herself in stone image there. Arru and Nyamba fought at Broy Amrangarri (the fighting place). Nyamba was chased away and painted herself as Nyamba Modengarri (with broken rib) at Yalinji. A group of snakes went to Nyalanggunda, the head place of the Mandangarri whose *yarriwada* (totem) is Manda, the gum of the kurrajong and the saliva of the snake. Plate 6 shows the snakes painted at the Mandangarri place. To the west, on Manning Creek, one of the snakes who had come with the rest to the Gibb River is finally painted (Plate 16). It is Wunggadinda, and her painting is Gulanwingangarri, of the one who was burned. She is shown pushing the spirit child out of the bush fire.

Crocodiles, kangaroos and dingoes are painted in the same way as Wandjinas, in outline with decorations on a white ground. At Budbunjoningarri, Manangurr the crocodile set fire to the bush and burned the people so badly that they had to cover their bodies with bark. He is painted there in the great jaw of a reptile's head rock (Plate 5). At the same place, but on a separate rock outcrop, are two kangaroos painted in company with Wojin and Dumbi the owl whose cruel injuries led the Wandjina to kill the people at Dumbai. The kangaroos have gentle expressions, with large eyes heavily lashed, making them look rather surprised and alert. The great red kangaroo, Yahmarro, and his wives have the same expresion far away in Lejmarro. Their eyes, too, are shown as though from the front, although their heads and bodies are in profile (Plates 2, 3). The story of Yahmarro was told in Chapter 3, but the painting itself is an unusual one, with Yahmarro's large body completely filled in with red ochre except for his head and front legs which are in normal outline style. He is actually being carried by Wahmaj Muli Muli in the way a hunter brings back a slain kangaroo across his shoulders. This idea is conveyed by framing the Wandjina's head in the curve between Yahmarro's front and back legs, keeping the classical full-face view of Wahmaj and the profile of the kangaroo. One of the Wandjina's sons, at the head of Yahmarro, is painted over an earlier figure of what looks like a bird. This, too, has both eyes shown on a head drawn in profile. Four more sons of Wahmaj Muli Muli are painted under a rock ledge opposite the main shelter (Plate 4). They are composed in a way similar to that at Wanalirri, with three of them superimposed, upright, over one which lies full-length along the rock. Like the snake paintings at the Mandangarri place, these are fresh and bright, suggesting that they have been retouched more recently than many others. However, it is possible that all of Wahmaj's sons were painted later than the original Yahmarro scene, for none exhibit the same detail or fine, painterly touch as the rest and one is superimposed over an older figure painted Yahmarro style.

Near a spring in the Napier Range, two large dingoes wait in a shallow cave to jump on a kangaroo as it comes to drink (Plate 13). They, like the kangaroos, are shown in profile while their eyes remain in full-face view. Their outlines, on a white ground, are filled with series of close marks to indicate hair, but the heads are marked off from the bodies and each tail has a curious knob at the end. In each case a feature is made of the anus and this parallels the treatment of some of the grotesque figures at Wanalirri. There a host of figures crowd around the edges of the main Wandjina compositions. There are figures recognisable in nature: snakes, lizards, Dumbi the owl, as well as a number in human form. One of these is Ngonol, spirit of the wind and cyclone (Plate 9) who is very reminiscent of some of the Quinkan-style figures of Cape York (Plate 36). Next to Ngonol is a grotesque figure — hardly human — who is described as Juwa, an evil spirit or devil. Like his companions and like the dingoes, his anus is greatly emphasised and he is said to crush children's heads with rocks. Djuari is the name given by Crawford for the figures of the spirits of the dead — ghosts which are always to be avoided. His illustration of Djuari painted at Wyndham is in the same style as a figure seen at Kunanurra. A pair of grey and red human figures hover on the rock wall at the western end of Wanalirri shelter (Plate 10). They give the strongest impression of women giving birth but were described as lightning spirits who, while having Wandjina-style heads, were 'not really Wandjinas'.

There is, in Kimberley, a series of rock paintings which is acknowledged to be older than the Wandjina style and to belong to a separate artistic tradition. These are referred to as Brad-

A Juwa spirit of the dead painted at Kunanurra, Kimberley.

shaw figures, named after Joseph Bradshaw, an explorer who sketched some of the figures when he travelled through Kimberley towards the end of the last century. Bradshaw figures are quite small, lithe and graceful, often elegant and shown dancing or running in scenes with many figures. Their similarity to the Mimi figures of Arnhem Land is very obvious, especially since both Bradshaw and Mimi figures are always painted in red silhouette and great detail is shown of weapons, implements and items of regalia such as headdresses, belts, armlets and so on.

One of the reasons that Bradshaw's name has adhered so well to the Kimberley figures is that the people say they know hardly anything about them. They are often described as 'rubbish' paintings, of no value to the people and unworthy of their attention. Since no man would gain prestige from painting them, he would waste his time by doing so. At Kalumburu, Crawford was told that the paintings were done by a small bird which, when it saw people or bush spirits, would hit its beak on a rock until it drew blood and, using this, would paint their picture. Sometimes bush spirits ask the bird to paint for them. Only in a place in southwest Kimberley did a man relate a story, about a grasshopper, to a Bradshaw figure.

Recently, Crawford has proposed that, while Wandjina and Bradshaw styles are distinct in

Bradshaw figures from Crawford, I. M., *The Art of the Wandjina*, p.84.

their classical forms, there may be good reason to believe that the newer style evolved in a natural artistic way from the older style. He shows not only Wandjina style paintings superimposed on Bradshaw figures, but also figures showing elements of both styles which have been painted on top of classical Bradshaw figures. It is interesting, at least, to look again at Plate 9, Ngonol the spirit of the wind and cyclone, who is not painted in the accepted Wandjina style, except for his face, and does resemble Bradshaw figures in some ways. He is small, graceful in attitude, painted in red silhouette and has fine decorative detail around his head. The fish in Plate 17 is superimposed over stick-type figures in red silhouette.

It seems that the artistic tradition marked by the Bradshaw figures, as well as the knowledge and custom associated with it, may well have been supplanted over time by the Wandjina forms. The great range of figures, intermediate between the two classical styles, indicates that it is was not a sudden change. Archaeological evidence is being brought to bear on this interesting study, and the links across the north of Australia for the Bradshaw style, those to the south for intermediate styles and the more localised nature of the typical Wandjina style are all being examined. Crawford feels that if this changing pattern is confirmed, the complexity of the Aboriginal past will be even greater than previously documented.

## Cape York

The place is spectacular in more than one way: a great wild mass of sandstone, gorges, rivers and forests sweeps westward from the coast to the Palmer River, hides the tiny township of Laura and forces on the hardiest visitor a sense of insignificance. To stand on a high ridge there in command of an endless vision of ancient strength is not to feel powerful. As in Kimberley, there, too, the wets have succeeded the dries for more time than we know. We do not know, either, how many of them have passed since ochre was used to make the first of the thousands of painted figures that crowd some of the great sandstone shelters in that wild place. But the country and the paintings make it satisfactory, somehow, that we may never know this and a great many other things.

The peoples of that place, the Gugu-Yalanji, Gugu-Imudji, Gugu-Warra, Gugu-Bullanji, Gugu-Minni and others, had hardly seen a foreigner until 1873. In that year gold was discovered on the Palmer River and there was one of the swiftest and most violent invasions of tribal lands ever recorded in Australia. Gold-fever sent tens of thousands of desperate men swarming up from the south. The foreigners had not come to settle and had not even settlers' erratic perception of the usefulness of peaceful relations with the people of the land. Clashes led to indiscriminate killing on both sides and

51

then to massacres of entire tribal groups of men, women and children. Some of the remnants of the people came to live on the fringes of the mining towns and, later, the missions, where they brought up a different generation of children. A few remained in the hills where some of them painted their new foes on the shelter walls. But they could not sustain their way of life; they died out, their passing perhaps speeded by the devastating wave of pneumonic influenza of 1922.

Hundreds of painted shelters have been rediscovered since 1960 by P. J. Trezise in the great sweep of country surrounding Laura (Plates 29-37). They were mostly living shelters. Nobody has lived in them for many years, but they are full of life. The birds, animals, spirits and people burst with colour and jostle for position, one on top of the other, on walls and ceilings. The empty space is on the floor where the fires used to group the people. In almost every place there are stencils where the paint has been sprayed from mouths over hands, feet, woomeras, boomerangs, axes and spears. Who knows why? You look, and you know that someone's hand was there — on that exact spot — at a time when its owner knew the answers to all those questions that foreigners ask of the silent figures in the shelters.

There are crocodiles, snakes, wallabies, birds with clutches of eggs, and people — lots of people — men and women, looking important or strange. You cannot help putting the names to them; they seem so reasonably to represent these things. Other shapes are more difficult to relate to known things. This is a dilly-bag, it is said, that a coffin, or a phallus. No, it is a catfish now — it was a phallus before only because it was painted close to a scene of group copulation.

There are many, many figures painted in only one colour, often red. They are silhouettes, completely bare of all decoration and features that do not show beyond the outline. They are shown with arms outflung and legs flexed, but they hardly ever actually move. You cannot imagine them frozen at a moment of running, dancing, gesticulating, or even watching. Some of them do seem caught at a moment of action, and these are almost always human figures. But often even those with eyes do not seem to notice anything, and a discernible expression is rare. The impression of movement is strong only when you first come in sight of the throng of figures. They seem, at first, like a huge cast of actors, all trying to up-stage one another. The waving arms of men and women quickly draw attention away from the quiet creatures who creep beside them or get in front of them. Someone's face is obliterated by the sweep of a hand. Those with bright colours or elaborate decoration seem to slip into the foreground in a riotous perspective created by relative size and superimposition.

Sometimes, the absorbed bodies of ancient creatures make an intricate landscape where newer figures now live (Plate 36). Some of these newer figures insist on being recognised as really new: there are horses, some carrying men with guns. The men are painted in a way which suggests that they are wearing clothing: hats, boots and shirts. There have been a few figures recorded which have 'X-ray' features, and almost all figures seem to have been painted singly. There are some which suggest they may have been made at the same time, in pairs or slightly larger groups, but they are usually not related in a composition. Very few groups have been recorded which suggest that they are related in this way, although one particular 'fertility' scene suggests this very strongly, as does a row of flying foxes at the Split Rock site.

Almost all the recording and published work on the rock art of Cape York has been done by P. J. Trezise who has asked two basic kinds of questions. Of the Aboriginal people who have been taken by him to some of the sites he has asked, 'What is it?', and of the literature on rock art generally he has asked, 'How can I divide it up into styles?'

From the two sets of answers, he has developed two ways of labelling all the 1800 figures he has recorded. The 'What is it?' question yielded two kinds of information. In identifying a subject as, for instance, a rock wallaby, an informant may also state that the reason for painting it was that it was a totemic ancestor, or that painting it was an aid in catching it. This fused the what and the why and also, apparently, linked up with style which was defined in terms of colour and technique.

Six styles are proposed: stencils, outline drawings, dry pigment in outline and silhouette, monochrome silhouette, bichrome silhouette, and polychrome silhouette. The 'motive force behind a particular painting by a particular artist' was found to be of nine kinds: ancestral culture hero, totemic ancestor, spirit figures, sorcery, love magic, hunting magic, mortuary, weapons and implements, and stencils. Every figure could be labelled with one of the styles and almost every figure could be given a motivation, or reason, for existence. The motivation given for a particular figure interpreted by an Aboriginal informant could be transferred to

Cape York landscape.

other figures seen only by the recorder on the basis that they fitted the visual description noted for the first figure. But some of the 'motivations' listed are, in fact, visual descriptions. 'Sorcery' and 'love magic' may be reasons for the painting of some figures, but 'spirit figures', 'weapons and implements' and 'stencils' are descriptions of what is painted. 'Stencils' even occurs in both lists. This simply reflects the fact that ways of seeing and classifying rock art are still being developed.

Many of the stories from Cape York have been recorded by Trezise, and he retells some of them in his book *Quinkan Country*. The beings and the places of their stories often flow down the eastern side of the peninsula and up the western side. Although some of the old men who told these stories have been taken to painted shelters it has apparently not been possible to properly link individual figures of ancestral beings with particular stories. The old informants, from various places on the peninsula, have kept alive much of the oral tradition by hearing and retelling the stories, but they have apparently lost touch with the paintings and cannot reconnect the two forms in any detail.

The Palpalpi or Yadgabulla sisters travelled the country long ago. Their story is still told and their final images as granite masses are still pointed out but, although it is probable that they are painted in more than one place, no female ancestral figures now carry their name. Goorialla the rainbow, Gaiya the giant devil dingo, Ngalculli the red kangaroo and many others have their places and images in the country but no painting can be said definitely to represent them. Some spirit figures are called Quinkans; the name has been given to a series of painted shelters — the 'Quinkan Group Gallery' — and has come to characterise the country and the culture as far as outsiders are concerned. Quinkans seem to belong to folklore. Some of them are said to be very thin, and so pictures of thin people in the shelters have come to be called Quinkans.

Dick Roughsey (Goobalathaldin), a Lardil man of Mornington Island which is in the Gulf of Carpentaria some 550 kilometres west of the Laura area, visited some of the painting sites with his friend Trezise and old Toomacalin of the Olkula people who lived west of the Great Dividing Range. While they were camped near some engraved and painted shelters in the high, rough country of the Divide, Goobalathaldin remembers Toomacalin sleeping most of one day because he had had a bad night worrying about the *quinkans*. These are described as the evil spirits of the country who might try to steal a person's kidney fat. Toomacalin had seen a white shape out on the edge of the firelight and told his companions that a *quinkan* was watching him. Joe, a taipan-snake language man who had mustered cattle there along the upper Hann, told him that it was only a tall ant-bed. But old

Toomacalin knew how clever the *quinkans* are at making themselves look like a stump or an ant-bed. Goobalathaldin remarks that the *quinkans* of many people that Toomacalin had known in his early life were wandering that part of the country: while on their way to the camp the old man had pointed out a low timbered sandridge where he had helped bury his father many years ago. Quinkans, it seems, are the ghosts of the dead which, like the Juwa, or Djuari, of Kimberley, are feared and avoided.

Goobalathaldin later put together the information he had been told about the Quinkans to write a story book for children which he illustrated using the Quinkan figures painted in the rock shelters as models. This tells of some children who were lured away from their parents by the evil Imjin Quinkans, ugly creatures with claws and sharp teeth, their long penises transformed, in the children's story, into knobbed tails. The children's fate was due to be quite awful, but the Imjins' nasty plans were noticed by the tall, slim Timara Quinkans who watched, easily hidden behind the trunks of the slenderest trees, and eventually rescued the children by engaging the grotesque Imjins in battle. The central figure in Plate 29 may be an Imjin Quinkan.

Old Toomacalin was with Goobalathaldin, too, when the Lardil man was painting the story of Thuwathu the rainbow serpent on a bark. This story, as told by Goobalathaldin, was related in Chapter 2, and it was told to Toomacalin who said that his people, the Olkula, kept the Rainbow legend. Their name for him was Goorialla, and part of his story place was on the Desert Plateau nearby. The plateau is a watershed with rivers flowing out from it in all directions, and these had been made by different kinds of snakes as they crawled away to escape a terrible magic fire set long ago by the bird people. The bird people wanted to destroy the snake people because of a quarrel between them, and old Toomacalin told of some 'bad business' he himself had had not so long before with 'Old Rainbow'.

Toomacalin had been fishing on the Morehead River, one of those made by the snakes in that distant time, when something enormous took his line. A mighty fight followed in which Toomacalin was almost pulled into the water several times. Eventually, with a great heave, the creature came up — and looked at his captor with huge green eyes. Toomacalin, with a shock of realisation, quickly cut the line, hoping that the Rainbow would forgive him. But no, Goorialla appeared soon in the sky, sending a mighty

A row of what look like yam figures painted at Guguyalanji Main Camp shelter, Cape York.

thunderstorm crashing down on the people who barely escaped being drowned in the floodwaters that quickly rose.

Goobalathaldin has also written and illustrated for children an old story of Goorialla, presumably as told by the old Olkula man. The Rainbow, as we have seen, travelled in many northern places, leaving his story places in the country of many different peoples and his name in their languages and knowledge.

Percy Trezise has spent many years tramping through the wild country in southeast Cape York. He has recorded the rock art by means of a portable grid and, of course, on film. Where possible he has taken Aboriginal informants to see the figures and attempt interpretations of them, but those who had lived in the bush were already old men in the 1960s. Captain Trezise recalls that he was fortunate to get a few of the remaining old men to accompany him to some of the galleries where they attempted an interpretation of many of the paintings based on their knowledge of tribal lore and custom. They identified a kangaroo-type painting as being definitely a rock-wallaby by the shape of its feet, and pointed out paintings of objects they were convinced were bark coffins, or dilly-bags. This does not give the impression that the old men were very familiar with the way in which the objects were depicted, although they felt they recognised them. They also separated the 'good' figures from the 'bad', the 'good' being paintings of culture heroes, totemic and ritual increase figures, and the 'bad' being some spirit figures or

Quinkans, sorcery or death magic paintings and love magic paintings.

Although Captain Trezise has recorded information and stories from many places in the north of Queensland, he points out that Cape York was not such a fortunate place for anthropologists as Arnhem Land, which was settled in a reasonably peaceful manner, leaving the tribal people in a position to tell of the paintings and other art forms which were still part of their living culture. In Cape York, the stories that are still known and told do not seem to relate directly to the painted figures in the great galleries which are not matched in any way by the few other instances of rock art on the peninsula. The importance of particular figures can only be judged by the time and skill spent in their painting because their names and their places in local knowledge are not known.

Still, whether or not individual ancestral and totemic figures have been painted by selected, trained and accomplished artists and the secular sorcery, love and hunting magic figures were made by those with lesser skills, as Captain Trezise suggests, they all manage to overcome their differences when they are seen tumbling in great crowds over the ochre-soaked walls and ceilings. Whatever reason any one of them has for being there will largely remain secret, but more people than their artists knew existed can now take in their extraordinary visual image. That, at least, remains and is informed in general terms by the stories of the country.

## Arnhem Land

Each year the great wet spreads sheets of gleaming water across the plains, fed by rushing torrents which sometimes sweep over the floors of caves and shelters. From above, in the mighty escarpments, the water descends in rushes and trickles, falling straight to the ground from the overhangs which hide the shelters. Sometimes there is more water than usual and the angle of the rocky overhang is not enough to send it straight to the ground: it rushes into the shelter and down the inside walls. Then it washes over figures painted in ochre and turns floors where people once lived into muddy pools.

But there are many, many places weathered out of the bases of the massive escarpments. Many of them are large, dry shelters, and in some of these — still a great many — people spent the wet season. Often the walls and ceilings of the living places carry painted pictures of the beings who helped to make the land and the

law, of the people themselves and of the animals, birds and fishes which were their responsibility and their sustenance. Contact with peoples of other lands is recorded in the paintings: Macassan praus, European sailing ships and steamers, guns, knives, buffaloes and other animals introduced recently. In the Wellington Range, near the central north coast of Arnhem Land, paintings show all these things. At one place a Macassan dagger in its sheath which has been painted in the X-ray style with a red ochre outline and interior design on a white ground keeps company with a huge saltwater crocodile and a giant lotus lily plant.

At this place, too, the debris on a shelter floor contains animal bones, shells and burial remains, and a scatter of glass fragments, including a piece of Chinese porcelain. Farther south, in a secluded valley, Aboriginal people of the area have identified a silhouette painting of two people with wide hats in a cart or other vehicle with lines running underneath it as a record of the construction by Chinese workers of the Pine Creek-Darwin railway in 1886-89. The ships which sailed up the South and East Alligator Rivers increasingly from 1818 still sail across the rock in many places. Steel axes are stencilled and Macassan tobacco pipes protrude from the mouths of painted people. A shelter in the Hawk Dreaming area has, besides a steel axe, a central painting of a ship complete with sails, cabin and portholes, a cowboy in wide hat

Arnhem Land landscape.

and other clothing, a cat and a picture of the Sydney Harbour Bridge.

This brings the rock art tradition in Arnhem Land very much 'up to date' in a most unexpected way. But the recent tradition of 'contact' paintings is only a small part of the total recent rock art expression. A series of fish in the X-ray style, as good as the best in the tradition, was painted in 1964 at the Nangaloar Gallery. There are three barramundi, a bream, a freshwater garfish, a saratoga and two catfish. In 1969, E. J. Brandl photographed Jacky Bunggarnial painting a crocodile at Cadell River, central Arnhem Land. Both of these paintings were, in a sense, 'commissioned' — outsiders asked the artists to paint them. In the case of the crocodile, the point was a demonstration of technique in mixing and applying pigments. Perhaps the most recent known painting that was done for traditional reasons is Mandarg's 1965 painting of Borlung, the rainbow snake. He made it because Borlung, the rainbow, lives in the rock at the Cadell River Crossing.

Although very few rock paintings in Arnhem Land are the work of living artists, or even artists clearly remembered, the tradition and its subjects are known still to quite a number of people even though settlers, traders, government authorities and missionaries moved the people from their country, making the painted shelters places to be visited rather than lived in. Pictures of the beings, creatures and events that influence peoples' lives — perhaps less now, or in a different way — are made today on bark, not rock.

But there are people who can tell the stories, and they have worked with many outsiders to record them, mostly as they relate to pictures on bark. The great stories of the creation have their places all over the country in the form of hills, gorges, waterholes, strangely shaped rocks, caves and shelters. The creator beings are often expressed in ochre on rock, but not necessarily in the sacred places themselves. A sacred site may have no art, and rock art sites are important in many different ways.

As far as we know, the earliest type of rock painting in Arnhem Land is what is known as 'Mimi art' (see Plates 43, 48). Most people say that it is the work of Mimi people or Mimi spirits — 'the old people', many say. There are lots of people in Mimi art; they run, dance and hunt in groups, their fine weapons at the ready and their many ornaments flying with them as they move. They are slender beings, often elegant, sometimes frantic and almost always active. Their lines and silhouettes are in one colour, usually one of the red ochre shades, and the figures are often said to have 'no meaning' to present people. This does not mean that weapons, animals and ritual paraphernalia cannot often be identified. Some people will even hazard a guess at the meaning of a Mimi scene. The goose-wing fans, the woomeras, spears and smaller goose spears are pointed out quite readily by some, while others, identifying animals in the scenes, may say that, nevertheless, they ought not be painted in that way. From the peoples' general reaction to Mimi art, E. J. Brandl concludes that its social and cultural significance changed and lessened as time passed.

Mimi art is probably the longest lasting rock art style in Arnhem Land. G. Chaloupka, who prefers 'Dynamic Figures' to Mimi as a style description, puts the start of this style well before 10 000 years ago, before estuarine conditions came to the Arnhem Land Plateau with rising sea levels. The length of the Mimi tradition is born out at this end of history at a number of places. At Red Lily Lagoon, near Oenpelli, a group of typical Mimi hunters is reported to overlie 'recent X-ray' paintings. Ideas like 'typical' and 'recent' are part of the analysis of the art which has produced information about it. The figures of people and animals in Mimi art are remarkably 'true to nature', but the composition of Mimi scenes is much more symbolic. Brandl suggests that the *arrangement* of figures carries meaning beyond that which can be seen and immediately understood. Certain animals are sometimes emphasised at certain places and are often larger than the people, suggesting mythical or totemic meanings for the scenes. The broad stylistic descriptions such as 'Mimi art' and 'X-ray art' can be divided, as Brandl has done, into 'Early' and 'Late', in the case of Mimi paintings, and 'Incipient', 'Simple', 'Standard' and 'Complex' for X-ray art. 'Incipient X-ray art' gives the clue to the theory that X-ray art grew from Mimi art, just as Crawford has suggested that Wandjina style art in Kimberley evolved in a natural way from the 'Bradshaw' figure kind of expression. Chaloupka's approach to style succession in these northern regions is different and just as interesting.

X-ray art is the kind that is believed to have been most recently made in Arnhem Land. Many people can tell of its subjects and the stories that belong to them. X-ray art, as a style, points out a shift in atention from things which are actually visible in nature — when creatures are alive — to things which are not visible in that way but are known to exist. The surface detail of fur, feathers or scales of earlier art gives way to internal details. However, if skeleton, heart, intestines, liver and so on are not explicitly painted it does not mean that the figure in question is not a part of the X-ray style. See Plate 41.

The Rainbow spans great lengths of time, much of the country and many expressions in art. It encompasses many forms, concepts and stories, and bridges the sexes. It has as many names as people speak languages and is one of the most important aspects of Aboriginal religion and society. There is one and there are many Rainbows. A mighty, bisexual Rainbow lives now beneath the earth; others, male and female, live in the earth in many places. Sometimes the Rainbow is a snake, sometimes a being with snake-like body, a being with features of several animals, or almost completely human in appearance. In some places, present-day ritual to do with the Rainbow is not to be shared or even seen by women — it is secret as well as sacred.

Jingana, the great rainbow, lives underground. Should he come, one day, to the surface a great flood will kill all the people in the world, the Rembarnga say. Borlung, with his headdress of black cockatoo feathers and his beard of flesh and cartilage, is less powerful than Jingana and lives at the surface of the earth. It is he that Mandarg painted in 1965 at the Cadell River Crossing. Borlung is not easy to understand, for it is said by others that Mandarg represented not Borlung, but Jingana, the mother, who is bisexual and wears the white cockatoo feather headdress and whose beard is of hair.

Jingana became hungry, long ago when men and women did not look as they look now, and swallowed all the people. Later, Jingana vomited them up in a transformed shape, in this act creating men and women as they are today. She grew two large eggs in her belly; from one came a son, Borlung, who had a snake's body, and from the other came a daughter, Ngalgunburi-jaimi, who looked rather like a fish. All this was told to Brandl by Spider Murululmi, a Ngalgbon man.

Ngaliod, or Ngalyod, is another Arnhem Land name for the Rainbow. At Djerlandjal Rock, near Mt Brockman, the Rainbow appears to have a kangaroo's head and a snake's body, is painted in dark red and belongs to the oldest tradition of painting in Arnhem Land. Balmanidbal told Brandl that it is possible for any snake to become the Rainbow. If a snake, instead of crossing a waterhole close to the surface, dives down into the depths, it is because Jingana tells it to stay down there. The snake then remains underground and becomes the Rainbow. At Dadbe, the people would not go with Brandl to the waterhole because, they said, the Rainbow would smell them, come up and swallow them and destroy the country. Near here there are small hollows in the rock, not unlike those that the Wandjina is said to have impressed in the rock in Kimberley when the earth was soft. Ngalyod the rainbow, the old mother of the Gunwinggu people, travelled throughout the country long ago. She had children, the first Gunwinggu people, and taught them how to live. She cared for them and provided for them, and punished them when they did not care and provide for each other. She made rules to protect the people from incest and dangerous behaviour, and the stories of her travels and deeds are related today round the peoples' campfires.

The Lightning-man belongs to the high clouds and shows his power during the wet season. He is Namaragan to some, Namaren, Marden, Ngaliur and Namarrkon to others. He has stone axes on his head, elbows, hands, feet and hips (Plate 41). When he throws these he makes the thunder. A line of lightning circles him and, where it strikes, hard, heavy lumps can be found in the ground which, having power themselves, are taken by the people to their camps. Long ago, as Namarrkon the lightning-man reigned in the sky, Marili the doctor-man lived on earth with his people, the Gunwinggu. Marili had been taken into the sky by spirits and there he had known Namarrkon and had been given special knowledge by him. He was able to call the Lightning-man to earth when he wished and it was he who took ochres to a cave and, after singing the special words taught him by Namarrkon, painted the figure of the Lightning-man on the cave wall. Such was Namarrkon's power when angered, that Marili used his own power to summon him only rarely and when the need seemed to him pressing. Namool, an old and frail man, came one day to Marili saying that his youngest wife, made restless by his inattention, had taken a young man as her lover. Namool was unable to punish either his wife or her strong young lover and was a laughing stock among his people. He was also causing their anger as long as this serious breach of the law went unpunished. In his cave, Marili took the grass Namool had brought him from the place where the lovers had lain and he sang as he formed it into the figure of Namarrkon. With twigs and pebbles he fashioned the thunder axes which he tied on with banyan string, singing into the figure the spirit of the Lightning-man. As

Namarrkon came to earth, the grass burned and the land blackened and Marili sang against the guilty lovers. The Lightning-man came upon the woman and the young hunter as they rested by a fire they had lit to cook a wallaby. He leaped forward, snatching the stone axe from his right knee. From his hand flashed a sheet of fire which blackened the hunter's face and burned his body. From his left knee he unleashed a bolt of fire at the woman's body, cleaving it as his terrible voice cracked through the bush.

In places around Deaf Adder Creek, the Lightning-man is painted in similar form to that on Plate 41. There, also, he has X-ray features and has been classed as 'Late' Mimi style. In the Cadell River area there is a painting of him in an earlier Mimi style. Here his form is different, showing a long body and shorter arms and legs. Stone axes sprout in profusion from his head, right elbow, hands, hips and feet. Like the Deaf Adder Creek paintings, and unlike that at Nourlangie, he has no facial features, and his genitals are small.

In a place at the base of Mt Brockman, a group of red figures in partial silhouette overlies similar figures in yellow ochre (Plate 45). Some show animal as well as human characteristics, suggesting perhaps totemic significance.

A group of very similar figures at a most important place not far away was described to Brandl, along with all the paintings, Mimi and X-ray, at that place, as put there long ago by Jingana the rainbow. The whole area is of great importance to the people, for the King Brown Snake has lived in a rockhole there since he was transformed into a Rainbow.

The profusion of fishes, animals, birds, reptiles and plants found in Mimi art but talked of more in recent X-ray styles, sometimes represents a number of ideas that are often brought together by outsiders and expressed as 'totemism'. It is a most difficult set of concepts for any non-Aboriginal to understand, but perhaps it could be said to be a way of thinking about and ordering the relationships between people, and between people and their entire environment. A man might point to the figure of a fish and say it is a painting of him; yams might stand to him in the relationship of father, another creature of mother. Everything in the world belongs, and the belonging is drawn in firm rules and celebrated as part of life.

Some older figures, as we have seen, seem to represent both people and creatures in one being. These are said to show the world's creatures before they were separated into people and animals by the special ceremony and fire made by Nagorgo, the father. Some such figures, when they have strange features such as twisted limbs or claw-like hands, or are bisexual, may represent malignant spirits or the images associated with sorcery rather than totemic concepts. Sometimes painted animal tracks symbolise the relationship of the creature to man rather than simply standing symbolically for the animal itself.

As in other places, spirit beings abound in Arnhem Land and most of those painted and talked about seem to be of the malignant variety. The Nadubi spirit people, according to Mountford, not only steal food from the camps but, much worse, shoot unwary travellers with the barbed spines that grow from their bodies. Usually people who encountered the Nadubi died. The Nabarakbia are dangerous, too, for they will extract the spirit of a sick person through the solar plexus then cook it and eat it, killing the victim. The Namorodo are known in Central Arnhem Land, where they both shoot people with the long nails from their claws and kill sick people. They may be the ghosts of people who were evil in their lifetimes and who now fly around at night.

Although much less is known about the figures painted in the Mimi style than about the X-ray art, the traditions may not be separate. They express, in ways that can be visually very different, essential aspects of the creation and the laws. The rock art of Arnhem Land perhaps shows the greatest variety of forms and styles of any region in Australia. As a body of art it is intensely interesting, being part of the traditional knowledge of many living people. The rock art, itself, is particularly beautiful.

## To the South

South of the three areas which link the top of the country from west to east lies, of course, the rest of Australia. There are rock paintings in places scattered all over the mountains, valleys, plains, forests, deserts and coasts of that huge, diverse terrain. Particular art sites show paintings which are as numerous, as diverse, as beautiful — and certainly as interesting — as specific sites in the far north of the country.

Behavioural scientists have found the paintings of the north fruitful because more people are found who carry knowledge of them and their place in societies and religion. The smaller amount of information collected from the huge number of people in the rest of Australia was written down longer ago and is much more 'patchy' geographically. There are many areas where the people who made and lived with rock paintings were never asked about them or any other aspects of their lives, areas where only now the descendants of the artists are 'discovering' the ceremonial places, the burial places and the art places of their forebears.

By and large, the farther south you move, the more often this is likely to be so, since whole tribes of people were moved off their land early in the European colonisation of the south and in some places, were wiped out completely. In the Sydney area, for example, six tribes were extinct within thirty years of European settlement.

The peoples of the central deserts are a notable exception to this. Although the different tribes were eventually all made to live in settlements, this happened to the last of them more recently since their country was much less attractive to settling farmers and graziers. Knowledge has been retained among the people who still — and more and more often — return to their own places in the huge country which ignores the boundaries of three new Australian States.

Uluru was one such place, steeped and clearly marked with dreaming knowledge and law, which, being also a spectacular and fascinating feature of the landscape, captured the imagination of many an explorer. Among them, C. P. Mountford was so impressed by the huge monolith of Uluru — Ayers Rock — that he set himself the task, in 1935, of finding out all he could about the people associated with the place.

By about 1940, Mountford had lived and travelled extensively with Pitjatjantjara people who were then following, undisturbed, their normal way of life. Although they were associated with Uluru and told its creation stories, none was 'of Uluru' in the strictest sense and it was not until 1960 that Mountford was able to go there with a man who had been fully initiated at Uluru.

He was a Mala (hare-wallaby) man, descendant of the great Mala creator-ancestor who rose from the empty land to travel and teach long ago in Tjukurpa times. In those times, Uluru rose out of a large, flat sandhill and, with the help of Mala and other creator-ancestors, it became as it is now and will remain forever. It is the spiritual and physical home of the Tjukurpa-beings' descendants. In Tjukurpa times, the Mala people had come from the northwest to Uluru to initiate their young men. Their approach to the place is now marked by an outcropping line of bare rock on the northwestern corner. While the elders and the youths conducted their

Flinders Ranges landscape.

ceremonies, the women and children were sent to Tabudja at the eastern end of Uluru where they spent the days gathering and preparing food for the men. All around there now are the rockholes, boulders and other features of the transformed Mala women and their children. On Tabudja's southern slopes, a low shallow cave where, during those creation times, the Mala nursing mothers sheltered, now contains the bodies of their infants transformed into small boulders on the shelter floor. The older women rest now as boulders on Tabudja's summit. At the base of Tabudja, an overhang in the rock was once the wet-weather shelter built by an old Mala man whose duty was to guard the women and make sure they did not see any of the special ritual being performed by the men. His watching body is there now, a long boulder at the overhang's mouth, and nearby some depressions in the rock mark the places where he urinated in the night. He danced to pass the time (Plate 18), making ceremonies with his

The transformed camps of the Mala men at Uluru (Ayers Rock), Northern Territory.

friends in places above the overhang, decorating his body in a windbreak now marked by a rock ledge. The Mala men guarded a precious eagle-chick, Kudrun, which played a part in their rituals. Strangely marked depressions in the rock (among them one known to outsiders now as 'the brain') are the transformed camps of the men whose duty it was to guard Kudrun. Above these places, the lines of caves were once the initiates, lying on the ground as they were decorated by the old men.

While the Mala people were carrying out their special ceremonies, the Windulka (mulga-seed) men from the west sent the bell-bird to Uluru with a message asking the Mala people to come to take part in one of their ceremonies. The Mala men were asked to bring Kudrun with them so that some of the eagle-chick's down could be used to decorate the dancers. The Mala men were angered and sent, instead of eagle-down, a parcel of white ash with a discourteous reply. Such an insolent message angered the Windulka men in their turn, and they instructed their doctor-men to create Kulpunya, a malignant spirit dingo, who would be sent to destroy Kudrun and the Mala people. A mulga branch made Kulpunya's backbone, a forked stick his ears. He was given teeth from the marsupial mole, a bandicoot's tail and women's hair along

his back. The doctor-men sang into Kulpunya the spirit of evil, sang their dreadful creation to life and, finally, sang into him hatred and malice towards all strangers. When it was all finished, Kulpunya was sent on his awful mission to Uluru.

Lunba, an old kingfisher woman, was camped at Uluru where she kept watch, for she expected an attack from the mulga-seed people. She kept a clear view of the surrounding country so that she could warn the Mala people if she saw anything suspicious, camping in places now marked by caves. One has a boulder at its opening, her transformed body resting in the sun, while her breasts are now rocky projections from the cave roof. Kulpunya came to Uluru in the middle of the day when everyone but Lunba was asleep and he paused right under her camp to raise his head so that he could see where the Mala men kept Kudrun the eagle-chick. Before Lunba could alert anyone, Kulpunya had found the eagle-chick and torn it in half and, leaping off, had attacked and destroyed all the women and children in the main camp and at Tabudja as well as the old men and initiates near Tjinindi rockhole on Uluru's northern edge. Rocks and boulders still mark their bodies.

Lunba fled to warn the men and youths on Uluru's western side. The Mala men gave the initiates the sacred pole which was dragged by them over Uluru to the southeastern side. As the young men tried to drag their ceremonial

Every feature of Katatjuta (the Olgas) is part of creation knowledge.

pole to safety, their feet left spectacular chasms on the northwest slopes. The sacred pole lies in image there still, a great column of rock between the chasms. Deep gutters were formed on Uluru's summit by the feet of the initiates, and others by the feet of the Mala men as they fled Kulpunya's terrible vengeance. With their ceremonial pole and accompanied by the old kingfisher woman, Lunba, the Mala men fled to the east, coming to rest at a spring called Oolra where, once again, they were attacked by Kulpunya.

In Tjukurpa times, too, the Kunia (carpet snake) people came to live at Uluru. Some of them camped by Uluru water in the great flat sandhill, a waterhole which is now on the top of the transformed Uluru rock. At that time a group of Liru (venomous snake) men were travelling about the country causing great trouble to the rest of the Tjukurpa peoples. They stayed at Katatjuta (the Olgas) and set out from there to attack the Kunia carpet snake people. Where their spears fell in the sand, numerous potholes are now to be seen in the rock. A large split boulder, hollowed into a cave, is the transformed body of Bulari, a Kunia woman who gave birth to a baby there. The baby is there still, a rock near the opening to the cave, as are the marks of the knees of the women who knelt to assist Bulari as the baby was born. Nearby is a painted cave (Plate 21) with two stones in front where Bulari once sat with her baby between her knees. From those times, women have come to this place to have their children. It is a special

place where the rocks of Bulari are rubbed smooth and shiny from contact with the women who seek her help in childbirth.

When the Liru men attacked her camp, Bulari took her newborn child in her arms and met them, spitting at them *arukwita*, the spirit of disease and death. This killed many of the venomous snakes. Still the Liru men attacked, causing the deaths of so many Kunia people that some of their grieving relatives sang the *arukwita* song to kill themselves. The bodies of the Kunia people were all changed into large and small boulders, and their hair into the fig trees that grow between them. Two of these stones, the bodies of the Kunia woman Ingridi and her husband, are increase stones for the carpet snake. Rubbed at the proper time and with a special song sung over them, the life-essence of the carpet snakes will leave them and go into the female snakes to increase their numbers.

Uluru, with its thousands of Tjukurpa events and people permanently recorded in its huge rock body, is just one of the more visually spectacular places of the peoples of the central deserts. Nearby, Katatjuta, too, has a dreaming story for every boulder, cave, water stain and bush. Unlike Uluru, there are no places where people painted in their shelters, although the rock has engraved designs in a few places. Other painting places are to be found in that huge country, although much less is known about

61

many of them. The paintings on the sheer rock sides of the Emily Gorge far to the northeast of Uluru (see endpapers) are said to be sacred symbols of Udnirringita (witchetty grub) people.

Out of the desert places of the great centre of the country, to the south, are many places where the earth receives more rain, where great rivers run between green banks to the coasts. There, on the grassy plains, in the bush and on the many shores, groups of people were not so scattered and sometimes did not move about as far or as often as their counterparts in the centre.

In rock shelters sometimes screened from view by high grass and thick stands of shrubs and trees, the people often stayed for a while, adding, from time to time, some painted figures to those already on the walls and ceilings. The hands of many, many people have been stencilled on the rock over an unknown period of time. There are what have been described as 'culture-heroes', large figures with imposing presence who dominate the creatures, people and other shapes painted round about. You can find groups or chains of stick-like people, animals you cannot help calling 'kangaroo' or 'lizard', and other figures which may stand for beings, things or ideas not to be understood except by drawing parallels over great distances.

In the west of what is now the State of New South of Wales, not far from the town of Cobar, there are shelters in which crowds of small stick figures bounce and jostle (Plates 25-27). They are painted on, round and about one another, sometimes upright, sometimes apparently falling about, even standing on their heads. They wave weapons, standing defiantly, hunt or seem to dance in rows across the rock. Sometimes they crowd in depressions, framed as though the rock was opening on a scene. Silhouetted emus, yellow and white, move away from hunters brandishing the weapons that may spell their doom. There are more human figures than any other kind; some even seem to fight each other with shields and clubs. Some are women, shown in groups with men, and sometimes the people appear to have headdresses. In some of the larger crowds, the longer you look the more you seem to see. The people are usually painted stick-fashion, some thinner, more reed-like than others. Some are joined in a tiered pattern, like netting, some join hands in rows and others are separate but often seemingly involved in action with other figures.

The animals are 'fatter', shown in silhouette without added decoration. They are painted in one of a number of colours, sometimes marching along amongst their own kind, sometimes part of the great melee of hunting and dancing. Usually, animals such as kangaroos and emus are shown in profile, while lizards are painted in plan, as seen from above, and people are in full-face view. There are figures which seem to represent tortoises, snakes, echidnas, dingoes and fishes, and nets may have been used in hunting some animals. Individual figures show little detail, but when the small figures come together in crowds, the scenes seem to teem with life and an impression of detail is created.

Although we have very little knowledge of the artists' intentions, it seems reasonable to suppose that they were varied. Some pictures were probably painted about the totemic links between people, animals and land, some perhaps as hunting magic. The figures themselves and their group activities are not unlike some of the Mimi art of Arnhem Land. Here, as anywhere else, we must be careful of assuming that everything has a reason for being there which has nothing to do with an artist's wish to paint something.

In a cave at Milbrodale in the Hunter Valley of New South Wales is painted a large red human figure whose arms reach across the rock in a great embrace of all before him (Plate 28). It is, indeed, a wide embrace, measuring over five metres from hand to hand. He has great white eyes and from under his arms radiate parallel lines of white which are reminiscent of those of the Ngonol cyclone figure in Kimberley (Plate 9). It is thought that he may be Baiamai, or Daramulun, the sky-being who was, with different names, the all-father of many southern peoples. His size, decoration and central position have led to this suggestion, though there is no one who can now say whether it is right or wrong.

Moving westward, into the range known as the Grampians in Victoria, there are a number of places where the often faint traces of an old way of life are to be seen. They are sometimes difficult to discern now and even more difficult to understand. In 1896, when the Reverend John Mathew read a paper on a painted shelter at Glenisla (Plate 24) to the Royal Society of Victoria, he noted that the oldest Aboriginals professed to have seen the paintings in their boyhood but that they were, by the 1890's, so unfamiliar with the place that they could not find it after a day's search. He says that the people of the area called themselves Kuli, but whether the old men with him were Kuli or not is not mentioned. However, he lists the subjects of the paintings: 'seven men engaged in a corroboree', 'a man and a woman', 'a wild turkey' and so on. No doubt he and the old men worked it out between them.

So far, there are only between thirty and forty painted sites recorded in Victoria, in the Grampians and the northeast of the State. Of these, according to F. D. McCarthy, the Glenisla shelter is the biggest and finest. Its figures are all in red, the animals in full silhouette and the people, while being of a stick-like form, are often fairly thick or rounded out to some extent, and even shown as full silhouettes. The small human figures often appear in motion and are reminiscent of the New South Wales figures — a point noted much earlier by the Reverend Mathew.

Other sites have mostly, or even all, white figures, but still only one colour is used for each figure. The animals suggested as depicted in the paintings include kangaroos, emus, snakes, dingoes, lizards and, at one site, fishes. Another site has an area of its cream-coloured, craggy wall covered by red-stencilled hands. More information on styles, colours and, possibly, subjects will come with further and more accurate recording of painted sites in the State.

Westward again into South Australia and up from the Lower Murray and Mount Lofty Ranges, through the Flinders Ranges to the Mann and Musgrave Ranges in the north, we come back towards the sort of symbolic representation by line and circle that we left in the central deserts. At Anthony's Hill, between Strathalbyn and Macclesfield in the south, some of the human figures are substantial silhouettes, brandishing objects in their hands, or carrying things on their backs. Others are long, attenuated figures, moving like reeds and often joined at the ends of their arms where hands might be. They are very like the slimmest of the western New South Wales figures. The fuller ones are reminiscent of those at Glenisla in Victoria.

At Yourambulla in the Flinders Ranges, lines take over in concentric U-shapes, radiating dashes forming circles, long parallel lines, 'combs' and double 'combs'. They are drawn in black, probably with charcoal, on the pinkish-cream rock. Further north in the Ranges, at Malkaia, there are more lines arranged in patterns, this time in white on a dark ground.

The people of the Flinders Ranges today identify themselves as Adnjamathanha — the 'hills people' — one of several groups once living in that country. The last full-blooded person of the original groups died several years ago and there has not been an initiation ceremony conducted since the late 1940s for a number of reasons. Three present-day Adnjamathanha, in an

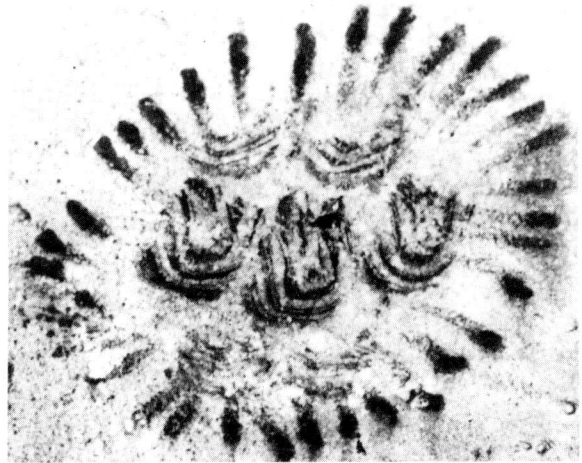

Yourambulla, South Australia.

Aboriginal view of the Flinders Ranges, have set down a number of creation stories. One of them may relate to the paintings at Arkaroo Rock, where two snakes crawl in parallel, meandering black lines past a pair of most unusual circular designs made on natural hollows in the rock (Plate 23).

The great, partly human beings were, at the beginning of the world, responsible for the creation of all the rivers, hills, mountains and gorges in Australia. Among the most beautiful of these places, as the Adnjamathanha know, are the mountain ranges now known as Flinders. To Wilpena Pound in those ranges came an old kingfisher man, Yulu Yulura, long ago. He came from the north and, at Leigh Creek, he lit a large fire to signal his approach to the people who were dancing and holding an initiation ceremony at Wilpena Pound. The charcoal left by his fire formed the coal deposits in that place.

Two huge Arkaroo snakes were also travelling south in the ranges and Yulu saw them as he passed through Brachina Gorge. He was frightened and crept behind some rocks to hide himself. Yulu and the Arkaroo snakes reached the Wilpena Pound ceremony at the same time. The snakes surrounded the people and swallowed them all except Yulu and Wild Turkey, who fled southwards, and a new initiate and a partly initiated man, who both escaped to the east.

The *vadnapa* man, who was partly initiated, became a stony hill near Wirrealpa Station. The *wilyaru*, newly initiated, man ran far over the edge of the country and was turned back by the people of that place towards Mt Chambers. He stopped when he could go no further and there, just south of the mountain, he turned into

Wilyaru Rock on the side of a small hill.

The Arkaroo snakes, so full of all the people they had eaten, lay down where they were and willed themselves to death. Their bodies now form the great walls of the Wilpena Pound and, so it is said, St Mary's Peak at the highest point is the head of the female Arkaroo.

In the wide southern areas of Australia there are many places like those in the Flinders Ranges where scattered, dispossessed Aboriginal people are bringing to a reforged cultural identity the stories, pictures and other things of their forebears. There are places like the Sydney-Hawkesbury region where nobody survived the extinction of whole tribes and great expanses of sandstone turn prehistoric pictures to new horizons. In the vast Centre, as in northern areas, pictures in many places belong with the rest of the knowledge of ways still walked, but walked now often in despair of the fact that nothing of former value seems sacred to any but a small handful of the recent invaders. Places, people and pictures: we have taken them all and put those whose value we can measure into our newer sacred places — laboratories, museums, art galleries, tourist resorts, smelters and banks.

# RECOMMENDED READING AND BIBLIOGRAPHY

## Recommended reading

Berndt, Ronald M. and Phillips, E. S., (eds), 1973, *The Australian Aboriginal Heritage: An Introduction through the Arts*, Australian Society for Education Through the Arts, Ure Smith, Sydney.

Flood, Josephine, 1983, *Archaeology of the Dreamtime*, William Collins Pty. Ltd. Sydney.

Maynard, Lesley, 1979, 'The Archaeology of Australian Aboriginal Art' in S. M. Mead (ed.), *Exploring the Visual Art of Oceania*, The University Press of Hawaii, Honolulu.

Mulvaney, D. J., 1975, *The Prehistory of Australia*, Pelican Books, Penguin Books Ltd, Ringwood, Victoria.

Roughsey, Dick (Goobalathaldin), 1971, *Moon and Rainbow: The Autobiography of an Aboriginal*, Seal Books edition 1977, Rigby, Adelaide.

Utemorrah, Daisy, Mowaljarlai, David, *et al*, 1980, *Visions of Mowanjum: Aboriginal writings from the Kimberley*, Rigby Ltd, Adelaide.

Wallace, P. and N., 1977, *Killing Me Softly: The Destruction of a Heritage*, Thomas Nelson (Australia) Limited, Melbourne.

## A select bibliography

Aboriginal Arts Board, 1979, *Oenpelli Bark Painting*, Ure Smith, Sydney.

*Aboriginal Sites in New South Wales*, 1979, National Parks and Wildlife Service, Sydney.

Allen, Louis A., 1976, *Time Before Morning: Art and Myth of the Australian Aborigines*, Rigby Ltd, Adelaide.

Berndt, Catherine H., 1979 *The Land of the Rainbow Snake*, Wm. Collins, Sydney.

Berndt, R. M. and Berndt, C. H., 1970, *Man, Land and Myth in North Australia: The Gunwinggu People*, Ure Smith, Sydney.

_____, 1977, *The World of the First Australians*, second edition, Ure Smith, Sydney.

Blainey, Geoffrey, 1975, *Triumph of the Nomads*, Macmillan, Sun Books, 1976.

Brandl, E. J., 1973, *Australian Aboriginal Paintings in Western and Central Arnhem Land*, Australian Institute of Aboriginal Studies, Canberra.

Bropho, Robert, 1980, *Fringedweller*, Alternative Publishing Cooperative Ltd, Sydney.

Chaloupka, George, 1980, 'From Palaeoart to Casual Paintings: Chronology of Arnhem Land Plateau Rock Art 17880 BP to 1973' unpublished MS, Museums and Art Galleries of the Northern Territory, Darwin.

Clegg, John, 1976, 'Sydney Rock Art', in P. Stanbury (ed.), *The Moving Frontier: Aspects of Aboriginal-European Interaction in Australia*, Reed, Sydney.

_____, 1977, 'The meanings of "schematisation" ' and 'A method of resolving problems which arise from style in art', in P. J. Ucko (ed.), *Form in Indigenous Art: Schematisation in the art of Aboriginal Australia and prehistoric Europe*, Australian Institute of Aboriginal Studies, Canberra; Gerald Duckworth and Co. Ltd, London; Humanities Press, New Jersey, USA.

Coutts-Smith, Kenneth, 1976, 'Cultural Colonialism', paper presented to Congress of AICA, Lisbon 1976, in *Artery*, 1976-77.

Crawford, I. M., 1968, *The Art of the Wandjina: Aboriginal Cave Paintings in Kimberley, Western Australia*, Oxford University Press, Melbourne.

_____, 1977, 'The Relationship of Bradshaw and Wandjina Art in north-west Kimberley', in P. J. Ucko (ed), *Form in Indigenous Art*, Australian Institute of Aboriginal Studies, Canberra.

Dallas, Mary, 1976, 'Aboriginal Art and Europeans', in P. Stanbury (ed.), *The Moving Frontier*, Reed, Sydney.

Edwards, Robert, 1974, *The Art of the Alligator Rivers Region*, Alligator Rivers Region Environmental Fact Finding Study, Canberra.

_____ (ed.), 1975, *The Preservation of Australia's Aboriginal Heritage*, Australian Institute of Aboriginal Studies, Canberra.

_____ and Guerin, Bruce, 1969, *Aboriginal Bark Paintings*, Rigby Ltd, Adelaide.

_____ and Stewart, Jenny (eds), 1980, *Preserving Indigenous Cultures: A New Role for Museums*, papers from a regional seminar, Adelaide, 10-15 September 1978, Australian Government Publishing Service, Canberra.

*Gallery of Aboriginal Australia*, 1975, Report of the Planning Committee, Australian Government Publishing Service, Canberra.

Groger-Wurm, Helen M., 1973, *Australian Aboriginal Bark Paintings and their Mythological Interpretation*, Australian Institute of Aboriginal Studies, Canberra.

House of Representatives Standing Committee on Environment and Conservation, March 1979, *Preservation of the Quinkan Galleries, Cape York*

*Peninsula*, Australian Government Publishing Service, Canberra.

Institute for the Conservation of Cultural Material, 1973, *Proceedings of the National Seminar on the Conservation of Cultural Material*, Perth 1973, C. Pearson and G. L. Pretty, (eds) ICCM, Canberra.

———, 1976, Proceedings of the ICCM National Conference, Canberra, May 1976, *Conservation in Australia*, S. Walston (ed.), ICCM, Canberra.

———, 1977, Proceedings of the International Workshop on the Conservation of Rock Art, Perth, September 1977, *Conservation of Rock Art*, C. Pearson (ed.), ICCM, Canberra.

———, June 1980, *ICCM Bulletin*, (ed.) W. R. Ambrose, The Australian National University, Canberra.

Isaacs, J. (ed.), 1979, *Australian Aboriginal Music*, Aboriginal Artists Agency, Sydney.

Kanytjurri Fox, Nancy, *et al*, 1979, *Tjuma: Stories from the Western Desert*, Aboriginal Arts Board of the Australia Council for Warburton Community Council Inc.

Lofgren, M. E., 1975, *Patterns of Life: The Story of the Aboriginal People of Western Australia*, Information Series No. 6, Western Australian Museum, Perth.

Maddock, Kenneth, 1974, *The Australian Aborigines: A Portrait of their Society*, Pelican Books, Penguin, Ringwood, Victoria.

Mathew, J., 1896, 'Note on Aboriginal Rock Painting in the Victoria Range, County of Dundas, Victoria' in *Proceedings of the Royal Society of Victoria*, Vol. ix (New Series).

Maynard, Lesley, 1977, 'Classification and Terminology in Australian Rock Art' in P. J. Ucko (ed.) *Form in Indigenous Art*, Australian Institute of Aboriginal Studies, Canberra.

McCarthy, F. D., 1974, *Australian Aboriginal Decorative Art*, The Australian Museum, Sydney.

———, 1979, *Australian Aboriginal Rock Art*, fourth edition, The Australian Museum, Sydney.

Mountford, C. P., 1965, *Ayers Rock: Its People, Their Beliefs and Their Art*, Seal Books edition 1977, Rigby, Adelaide.

———, 1976, *Nomads of the Australian Desert*, Rigby Ltd, Adelaide.

Nangan, Joe and Edwards, H., 1976, *Joe Nangan's Dreaming*, Thomas Nelson (Australia) Ltd, Melbourne.

Ovington, J. D. *et al*, 1973, *A Study of the Impact of Tourism at Ayers Rock—Mt Olga National Park*, Australian Government Publishing Service, Canberra.

Raggett, Obed, 1980, *Stories of Obed Raggett*, (in Pintupi/Luritja and English), Alternative Publishing Cooperative Ltd, Sydney.

Roughsey, Dick (Goobalathaldin), 1973, *The Giant Devil Dingo*, Wm. Collins (Australia) Ltd, Sydney.

———, 1975, *The Rainbow Serpent*, Wm. Collins, Sydney.

Rowley, C. D., 1970, *The Destruction of Aboriginal Society*, Pelican Books 1974, Penguin Books Ltd, Ringwood, Victoria.

Spencer, Baldwin and Gillen, F. J., 1899, *The Native Tribes of Central Australia*, reprinted 1938, Macmillan and Co. Ltd, London.

Stanbury, Peter (ed.), 1976, *The Moving Frontier: Aspects of Aboriginal-European Interaction in Australia*, Reed, Sydney.

Timaepatua, Mary Agnes, *et al*, 1977, *Kwork Kwork the Green Frog and Other Tales from the Spirit Time*, Australian National University, Canberra.

Trezise, P. J., 1969, *Quinkan Country: Adventures in Search of Aboriginal Cave Paintings in Cape York*, Reed, Sydney.

———, 1971, *Rock Art of South-East Cape York*, Australian Institute of Aboriginal Studies, Canberra.

——— and Roughsey, Dick, (Goobalathaldin), 1978, *The Quinkans*, Wm. Collins, Sydney.

Ucko, Peter J., (ed.), 1977, *Form in Indigenous Art: Schematisation in the art of Aboriginal Australia and prehistoric Europe*, Australian Institute of Aboriginal Studies, Canberra.

Widders, Terry, 1974, 'Aboriginal Rock Paintings: Politics and Ethics' in *Australian Natural History*, special supplement in Vol. 18, No. 3, The Australian Museum, Sydney.

———, 1976, 'Social Life: Aboriginal adaptations' in P. Stanbury (ed.), *The Moving Frontier*, Reed, Sydney.

Wilton, Christine, Coulthard, Clifford and Coulthard, Desmond, 1980, *The Flinders Range: An Aboriginal View*, Aboriginal Heritage Unit, Department for the Environment, South Australia.

# ROCK PAINTINGS
## OF ABORIGINAL AUSTRALIA

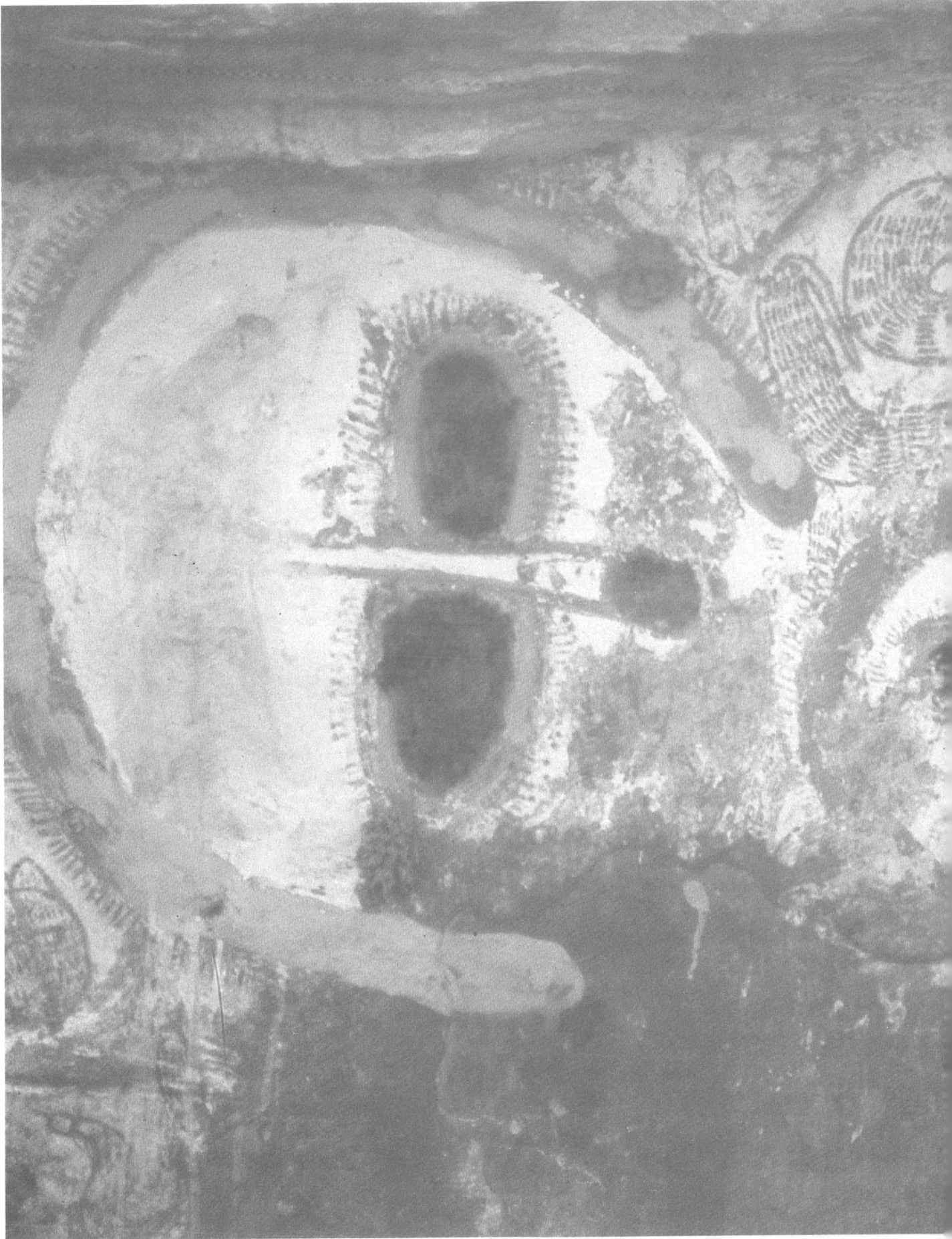

2 The Wandjina Warmaj Muli Muli carries Yahmarro the great red kangaroo, Lejmarro, Kimberley, Western Australia.

1 The Wandjina Warmaj Muli Muli, Lejmarro, Kimberley, Western Australia.

3 Yahmarro's wives and other Wandjina figures cluster behind him. The design beneath Yahmarro's tail represents kangaroo faeces. Lejmarro, Kimberley, Western Australia.

Above:
4  Warmaj Muli Muli's four sons look across at his painting. Lejmarro, Kimberley, Western Australia.

Right:
5  Manangurr crocodile images at Budbunjoningarri, Kimberley, Western Australia.

6   Wandjina and Galaru snake images at the Mandangarri Place, Gibb River, Kimberley, Western Australia.

Above:
7   The Wandjina Wojin, carrying a berry tree branch, is painted with his followers at Wanalirri, Kimberley, Western Australia.

Overleaf:
8   Wojin's followers at Wanalirri, Kimberley, Western Australia.

9    Ngonol cyclone spirit on left, with evil Juwa spirit,
Wanalirri, Kimberley, Western Australia.

10 Two lightning spirits at Wanalirri, Kimberley, Western Australia.

11  A pair of blackheaded rock pythons, Lejmarro, Kimberley, Western Australia.

12 Weather spirits: slim Winjin cyclone spirits and a storm figure on the left. Lejmarro, Kimberley, Western Australia.

13  Perilama or 'Dingo Spring', with the male dog
Yeddigee and the female Lumbiella, Napier Range,
Kimberley, Western Australia.

Right:
14  Nyararraman, the poisonous snake, Barker River,
Napier Range, Kimberley, Western Australia.

15   The Wandjina Rowalumbin, Barker River, Napier
Range, Kimberley, Western Australia.

16 Wunggadinda's snake image at Manning
Creek, Kimberley, Western Australia. She is
pushing the spirit child out of the bushfire.

17   Kunanurra, Lake Argyle, Western Australia. Fish
image painted over older sticklike figures.

18 Dancing Mala man, Uluru (Ayers Rock),
Northern Territory.

Left:
19  Geometric figures, Hunters' Cave, Uluru
(Ayers Rock) Northern Territory.

Overleaf:
20  Hunters' Cave, Uluru (Ayers Rock)
Northern Territory.

21  Bulari's Cave, known as Fertility Cave or Women's
Place at Uluru (Ayers Rock) Northern Territory.

22  Wombat Cave at Uluru (Ayers Rock) Northern Territory.

Left:
23  Arkaroo Rock, painting site of the Kingfisher man story, east-south-east of Wilpena Pound, Flinders Ranges, South Australia.

Above:
24  Glenisla, Grampians, Victoria.

Left:
25   Mount Grenfell, New South Wales.

Overleaf:
26   Mount Grenfell, New South Wales.

Left:
27　Mount Grenfell, New South Wales.

Above:
28　Large figure at Milbrodale, New South Wales,
may represent Baiamai, the all-father.

Left:
29  Split Rock, Cape York, Queensland. The middle figure is said to be a quinkan.

Overleaf:
30  Mushroom Rock, Cape York, Queensland.

32 Magnificent Gallery, Cape York, Queensland.

33  Magnificent Gallery, Cape York, Queensland.

Above:
34  Magnificent Gallery, Cape York, Queensland.

Overleaf:
35  Giant Wallaroo Gallery, Cape York, Queensland.

36   Giant Horse Gallery, Cape York, Queensland.

37 Coronation Hill, East Alligator River region, Arnhem Land, Northern Territory.

38  Nourlangie, East Alligator River Region, Arnhem
Land, Northern Territory.

39  Nourlangie, East Alligator River Region, Arnhem
Land, Northern Territory.

40  Obiri Rock, Arnhem Land, Northern Territory.
X-ray style painting of fish and what appears to be a
goanna.

41   Ancestral male and female figures, Namarrkon the lightning-man and spirit people, Nourlangie main shelter, Arnhem Land, Northern Territory.

42   Some of the figures in this shelter at Nourlangie may have been painted for purposes of sorcery or sympathetic magic. Arnhem Land, Northern Territory.

43 Mimi figures in red ochre at Little Nourlangie, East Alligator River region, Arnhem Land, Northern Territory.

44  Wallaby figure, Nourlangie, Arnhem Land,
Northern Territory.

Left:
45 Djidbi-djidbi, Mount Brockman, Arnhem Land,
Northern Territory.

Above:
46 Nourlangie, Arnhem Land, Northern Territory.
Hand stencil and two large figures, possibly insects.

Overleaf:
47 Nourlangie, Arnhem Land, Northern Territory.
Layers of painting with red fish and female figure.

48 Hunting Mimi figures at Obiri Rock, Arnhem Land, Northern Territory.